MOON UNDER HER FEET

MOON UNDER HER FEET

WOMEN *of the* APOCALYPSE

Kim S. Vidal

The Pilgrim Press
Cleveland

The Pilgrim Press ✦ 700 Prospect Avenue ✦ Cleveland, Ohio 44115-1100
pilgrimpress@ucc.org
www.pilgrimpress.com
(216) 736-3764

Grateful acknowledgment for permission to reprint from the following: ✦ Anonymous, "We Have a Dream." *Kalinangan* 12, no. 1 (1992). Used by permission of the Institute of Religion and Culture, Philippines. ✦ *Baker Encyclopedia of the Bible*, Walter A. Elwell et al., ed. Copyright © 1988 Baker Book House. ✦ Lynne Bundesen, *The Woman's Guide to the Bible*. Copyright © 1993 Lynne Bundesen. ✦ Leonard Davis, *The Philippines: People, Poverty, and Politics*. Copyright © 1987 The Macmillan Press Ltd. ✦ Vjosa Dobruan, *Testimonial Refugees: Others on the List Were Not as Lucky*. Used by permission of the U.S. Committee for Refugees. ✦ Julia Esquivel, "I Am No Longer Afraid of Death." Copyright © 1988 by WCC Publications. ✦ "ETAN to Protest Canadian Military Sales to Indonesia." Copyright © 1995 Peace and Environment Resource Centre. ✦ Elisabeth Schüssler Fiorenza, *Revelation: Vision of a Just World*. Copyright © 1991 Elisabeth Schüssler Fiorenza. Used by permission of Augsburg Fortress Press. ✦ Elisabeth Schüssler Fiorenza et al, ed., *Searching the Scriptures: A Feminist Commentary*, vol. 2. Copyright © 1993 by Elisabeth Schüssler Fiorenza. Used by permission of Crossroad Publishing. ✦ Colleen Fulmer, "Rest In My Wings." Copyright © 1989 Colleen Fulmer. Available from Loretto Spirituality Network. ✦ John Guimond, *The Silencing of Babylon: A Spiritual Commentary on the Revelation of John*. Copyright © 1991 John Guimond. ✦ Homer Hailey, *Revelation: An Introduction and Commentary*. Copyright © 1979 Homer Hailey. Used by permission of Religious Supply Center. ✦ Norma Hardy, "Women's Creed." Copyright © 1998 Norma Hardy. ✦ Pamela Harris, "Judy Marchand." Copyright © 1992 Westminster John Knox Press. ✦ Joyce Hollyday, *Clothed with the Sun*. Copyright © 1994 Joyce Hollyday. Used by permisson of Westminster John Knox Press. ✦ Andre B. Jacques, *The Stranger within Your Gates: Uprooted in the World Today*. Copyright © 1986 by WCC Publications. ✦ Martha Ann Kirk, "Women of the World." Copyright © 1990 Martha Ann Kirk. Used by permission of Loretto Spirituality Network. · Martha Ann Kirk and Coral Nunnery, "Cherishing the Earth." Copyright © 1989 Martha Ann Kirk and Coral Nunnery. Available from Loretto Spirituality Network. ✦ Penney Kome, *Women of Influence: Canadian Women and Politics*. Copyright © 1985 Penney Kome. Used by permission of Doubleday Books. ✦ Sr. Mary John Manazan, ed., *Women and Religion*. Copyright © 1988 Institute of Women's Studies, St. Scholastica College. ✦ Diann Neu, "Think Green: Hope for Planet Earth." Copyright © 1995 Women's Alliance for Theology, Ethics, and Ritual (WATER). ✦ Rene Parmar, "I Am a Woman." Copyright © 1988 by WCC Publications. ✦ Tina Pippin, *Death and Desire: The Rhetoric of Gender in the Apocalypse of John*. Copyright ©1992 Tina Pippin. ✦ Jean-Pierre Prevost, *How to Read the Apocalypse*. Copyright © 1991 Jean-Pierre Prevost. Used by permission of Novalis. · Debra Satz, "Markets in Sexual Labor." Copyright © 1995 University of Chicago Press. ✦ Pauline Viviano, "Huldah." Copyright © David Noel Freedman. Used by permission of Doubleday Books. ✦ Miriam Therese Winter, "Huldah," copyright © 1991 Crossroad Publishing; "One by One," copyright © 1987 Medical Mission Sisters; "We Are Always Starting Over," copyright © 1979 Medical Mission Sisters; *Woman Witness: A Feminist Lectionary and Psalter*, part 2, copyright © 1992 Crossroad Publishing; *Woman Word: A Feminist Lectionary and Psalter*, copyright © 1990 Crossroad Publishing.

Printed in the United States of America on acid-free paper

06   05   04   03   02   01   5   4   3   2   1

Library of Congress Cataloging-in-Publication Data
Vidal, Kim S., 1963-
     Moon under her feet : women of the apocalypse / Kim S. Vidal.
        p.   cm.
     Includes bibliographical references.
     ISBN 0-8298-1415-9
     1. Bible. N.T. Revelation—Criticism, interpretation, etc.   2. Bible. N.T.—Feminist criticism.   I. Title.
BS2825.2 .V53   2001
228'.064—dc21   2001021384

To
Karen Niven-Wigston
valiant ❧ persistent ❧ empowerer
in celebration of womanhood

Contents

Preface

While studying the book of Revelation at Union Theological Seminary in the Philippines in 1993, I was challenged by my former mentor, Professor Renate Rose, to consider as a course requirement the study of the women images of the book. Along with two divinity students, Rev. Ferdinand Serra and Rev. Marilyn Pascual, I developed a Bible study guide on women's issues based on several texts in Revelation. We successfully put together ten sessions, all contextualized to flesh out the situation of women in the Philippines. The study is a testimony to the struggles of these women in voicing their options for an alternative, reformed society. It affirms their convictions as they challenge the status quo and participate in creating a "new Philippines" that honors and upholds the dignity of women in all aspects of life.

In 1994, I immigrated to Canada and finished my degree in theology at St. Paul University in Ottawa. Affiliated with Wesley United Church, I am an active participant of Bamboo, a women's spirituality and social action group that strongly supports women's ministry and other contributions to society. With passion and determination, I shared the Bible study material with this group of empowered women, and I was able to get the group's approval to revise the contents. The writings of women theologians such as Elisabeth Schüssler Fiorenza, Tina Pippin, Susan Garrett, Joyce Hollyday, to name a few, have opened numerous learning avenues for me. The inspiring music of Colleen Fulmer, Carolyn McDade, Ruth Duck, and other composers, as well as the rich worship resources of Miriam Therese Winter, nurtured me spiritually. I was deeply encouraged to integrate their wisdom and creativity in the exploration of the themes. With the help of some members of Bamboo, the themes were elaborated to take into account women's situations in Canada, Latin America, Africa, and Asia.

I wish to thank Prof. Renate Rose, for sparking the flame in my deeper thoughts to write on the women images in Revelation. Thank you also to Prof. Elizabeth Dominguez and the Rev. Elizabeth Tapia, who helped me shape and develop an inclusive theology. I would like to thank my friend and classmate,

My sincerest appreciation goes to Pastor Karen Niven-Wigston, my spiritual adviser and confidante, for our unending discussions on issues that affect women in church and society, and for truly believing in me. I am deeply grateful to Susan Alter and Patty Kavcic for editing my work and providing me with inspiring wisdom in improving this material. I also want to thank Ava Kelly, Candice Magloire, Janet Thompson, and Linn Dodds for their creative input and enthusiasm in facilitating some of the sessions. A big thank you to the other members of Bamboo: Martha Garramone, Sally Duke, Donna Dowd, Anna Ibrahim, Amber Kelly, Jasmine Kelly, Laurine Pointen, Joy Cubar, Marma Vidal-Vizzari, Marlene Vetter, Yvonne Parker, and Linda Smith, for their invaluable time in sharing, brainstorming, discussing, and worshiping together.

My appreciation continues to the First United Methodist Church in Dagupan City, Philippines, and Wesley United Church in Ottawa for nurturing my faith and for encouraging me to experience the joy of community sharing.

My *pasasalamat* (gratitude) is extended to my Filipino friends: Edna Talosig-Monette, Evelyn Tan, Zony Wong, and Joseph Artienda for their spiritual reflections that helped me acknowledge the loving presence of God.

I also want to thank my professors and classmates at St. Paul University for creating in me a deeper faith dimension. The St. Paul Library is commended as well for its very rich resources and materials. I am truly grateful for all the authors, writers, contributors, musicians, and publishers who have allowed me to use their works in this book.

My sincerest thanks goes to Papang, Mamang, my brothers, sisters, nephews, and nieces for their guiding love and prayers.

My gratitude extends to Dad, Mom, and Jen for their invaluable support and concern.

Special thanks to my loving partner, Kenny Kim, for his technical assistance and for his constant encouragement to let me move on.

And to my wonderful son, Justin, for inspiring me and teaching me the meaning of motherhood.

I can touch the lives of other women as we journey together in solidarity.

Shalom and more power!

An Overview

The book of Revelation promises hope for a seemingly hopeless world. Its complex symbols and rich imagery challenge the reader to a deeper faith struggle. Its violent language assures that the "unjust" will receive punishment, but the "righteous" will be rewarded. While it expresses God's judgment, it also emphasizes the dichotomy of good and evil.

For many readers, Revelation emphasizes fear and destruction. In our churches today, few preachers use it as a scripture text for a sermon. The tormenting prophecies produce discomfort in looking at our present context in the light of sociopolitical and cultural conditions.

In spite of the tremendous disapproval of most readers, I find the Book of Revelation inspirational. It is a book that speaks of God's revolution against the oppressive dragons in our world. Applying the theology of John Dominic Crossan to Revelation pushes us to make a crucial decision: to choose between God and Caesar—God, being the symbol of "empowerment," and Caesar, "domination."[1]

To trace its historical account, the book was believed to be written during Emperor Domitian's reign from 81–96 C.E.[2] Christians during those times experienced a "great tribulation," a crisis related to religious, cultural, and political persecutions. According to Jean-Pierre Prevost, two important factors paved the way for the book to be written: the Christian community was seeking to define itself as a people of God in relation to its Jewish roots (ch. 2–11); and to courageously and openly state their position against the imperial power of Rome (ch. 12–20).[3] The book, therefore, was designed to arm the first century community of faith with God's unifying justice and "persistent resistance" against imperialism.

This Bible study material reflects the use of women images in the book of Revelation and offers a modest contribution for raising consciousness toward a theology of "persistent resistance" against political idolatry, all forms of oppres-

11

sion and exploitation, sexual and gender discrimination, degradation of human worth and dignity, and the destruction of the earth.

There are only four women images mentioned by the author of the book of Revelation (for the purpose of this study, I will be referring to "John" as the writer of Revelation). Three of these four images are metaphors: the Woman Clothed with the Sun, the Great Whore, and the Bride. Only one historical woman is mentioned, the prophetess "Jezebel," but her name has allusions beyond her known role in history.

Susan Garrett's interpretation of Revelation in the *Women's Bible Commentary* strongly emphasized that the language remains disturbing and dangerous because women are stereotyped as wholly good or wholly bad. The good are those whose sexuality is effectively controlled. They are women who do not question authority and prefer submission instead of resistance. The "good" metaphors are the woman clothed with the sun and the bride.

The wholly bad are those whose sexuality escapes management and manipulation. Obviously, these images include the Great Whore and Jezebel. These definitions might leave the readers confused and divided. They want to identify with the good but are reluctant to do so because the images deny self-determination. They hesitate to identify with the bad because of the strong social stigma attached to them, even though they may support the defiance of the "whores" against those who would control or destroy them. This imagery is dangerous because, intentionally or not, it promotes ethos in which women are discouraged to control their own bodies and their own destinies.[4] Violence against women in some cases is condoned, and this is a sad reality confronting women in their faith journey.

Primarily designed for use by women, this book can be offered to anyone who is interested in learning more about the female images in the Book of Revelation, or those who are supportive of women's issues and concerns. The suggested time frame for each Bible study is one-and-a-half to two hours, depending on the length of sharing and discussion. There are eleven sessions with the following themes: women's prophetic voices; women's opposition to war; women's leadership and empowerment; healing of prostituted women; the plight of "domesticated" women; women refugees; ecofeminism; and women's utopian vision. Hymns, songs, responsive readings, prayers, and suggested readings are included to enhance exploration of the issues.

Each Bible study uses the following format:

1. Objectives
This section presents the aims of the lesson.

2. Community Circle
This is generally composed of games, songs, and prayers to open up the session. Hymns and songs are suggested for the readers to use. It also deals with the telling of women's stories.

3. Biblical Text Exploration

In this section, some questions regarding the biblical text are open for exploration. Varied activities are also introduced to facilitate better learning and understanding of the text. It is suggested that the text is read before discussing or reflecting on the questions.

4. Contextualization

As the word suggests, this section is an application of the text to the current reality of women. Questions and activities are suggested for insight and reflection. This allows the participants or readers to share stories and experiences.

5. Responding in Faith

Creative activities are suggested in this section to gauge the reader's response to the challenges offered by each session.

6. A Moment of Reflection

A simple worship composed of suggested hymns/songs, readings, and prayers wrap up the session or individual devotion time.

7. Session Assessment

The evaluation of the material used in each session.

The facilitator may first need to go through all the study materials to get an overview of the material covered. Individual users of this resource may read at their leisure. To prepare for each lesson, the facilitator must be up-to-date on women's issues and understand the level of awareness of the participants. The facilitator must be well-informed with sociopolitical, economic, cultural, and religious trends that are helpful in discussing the themes. Reading the texts and letting them speak to our context will motivate the facilitator to encourage the participants as they go through a spiritual learning journey.

The participants, on the other hand, must be willing to contribute to the discussions by providing creative responses and sharing of experiences. It is suggested that individual readers have a journal or pad available to write answers to questions and/or their musings. It is of the utmost importance that an atmosphere of acceptance be created in group settings. Everyone's viewpoints, strengths, and limitations are to be recognized and heard. It is also suggested that current women's issues and biblical texts encountered by the participants in his or her personal study be offered to the group to enrich the overall experience.

Lastly, praxis is important! When we realize how significant these issues are in promoting global awareness of women's liberation, we should readily extend our support and concern to all women. Remember, learning is nothing without action! Cooperation, participation, and readiness in achieving the objectives are crucial in attaining the aims of this Bible study material. May this be a step toward a more meaningful journey of building solidarity!

Moon under Her Feet

Session I

Women of the Apocalypse

Objectives

➤ To discover the meaning of the different images of women in the book of Revelation.

➤ To understand the plight of women in our present world and the causes of their condition.

➤ To learn some ways to empower women.

Community Circle or Individual Centering

OPENING SONG

"Kumbayah" (traditional) or

"We Are One" (words: Doreen Larkshear-Smith, 1888; music: Jeeva Sam, 1987; arr. David Kai, 1995) or

"We Gather Here" (words and music: Bryan Jeffrey Leech, 1984) or

"We Are Gathered" (words and music: Miriam Therese Winter, 1982)

OPENING PRAYER
(privately or corporately)

O God of Revelations,
whose love and compassion extend to women of all times and ages;
assemble us (me) in this place,
with the hope that we (I) may have the wisdom
and the power to seek
your justice in our changing time.
Through Jesus, the Christ. Amen.

OPENING UP

Share or reflect on personal views on the book of Revelation by answering one of the following questions:

❧ What do I know about Revelation?

❧ How do I feel about the images it depicts?

❧ What is the message of the book?

❧ Wrap up the discussion by focusing on the objectives of this session using the material on page 1 as a point of reference.

Biblical Text Exploration
BACKGROUND

The images of women in Revelation were not created to advance the cause of women but to convey the "persistent resistance" message to seven churches. The female characters in these biblical texts and the female readers of today have one thing in common: they are both victims of an unjust social system. In this session, we will begin to examine the four images of women—the prophetess "Jezebel," the Woman Clothed with the Sun, the Great Whore, and the Bride—in a more challenging and inspiring light.

Read

Divide the participants into four groups, each with a particular female image to explore.

Group 1: The Prophetess "Jezebel"—Revelation 2:20–23

But I have this against you: you tolerate that woman Jezebel, who calls herself a prophet and is teaching and beguiling my servants to practice fornication and to eat food sacrificed to idols. I gave her time to repent, but she refuses to repent of her fornication. Beware, I am throwing her on a bed, and those who commit adultery with her I am throwing into great distress, unless they repent of her doings; and I will strike her children dead. And all the churches will know that I am the one who searches minds and hearts, and I will give to each of you as your works deserve.

Group 2: The Woman Clothed with the Sun—Revelation 12:1–6, 13–17

A great portent appeared in heaven: a woman clothed with the sun, with the moon under her feet, and on her head a crown of twelve stars. She was pregnant and was crying out in birthpangs, in the agony of giving birth. Then another portent appeared in heaven: a great red dragon, with seven heads and ten horns, and seven diadems on his heads. His tail swept down a third of the stars of heaven and threw them to the earth. Then the dragon stood before the woman who was about to bear a child, so that he might devour her child as soon as it was born. And she gave birth to a son, a male child, who is to rule all the nations with a rod of iron. But her child was snatched away and taken to God and to his throne; and the woman fled into the wilderness, where she has a place prepared by God, so that there she can be nourished for one thousand two hundred sixty days.

So when the dragon saw that he had been thrown down to the earth, he pursued the woman who had given birth to the male child. But the woman was given the two wings of the great eagle, so that she could fly from the serpent into the wilderness, to her place where she is nourished for a time, and times, and half a time. Then from his mouth the serpent poured water like a river after the woman, to sweep her away with the flood. But the earth came to the help of the woman; it opened its mouth and swallowed the river that the dragon had poured from his mouth. Then the dragon was angry with the woman, and went off to make war on the rest of her children, those who keep the commandments of God and hold the testimony of Jesus.

Group 3: The Great Whore—Revelation 17:1–18; 18:9–17a

Then one of the seven angels who had the seven bowls came and said to me, "Come, I will show you and the judgment of the great whore who is seated on many waters, with whom the kings of the earth have committed fornication, and with the wine of whose fornication the inhabitants of the earth have become drunk. So he carried me away in the spirit into a wilderness, and I saw a woman sitting on a scarlet beast that was full of blasphemous names, and it had seven heads and ten horns. The woman was clothed in purple and scarlet, and adorned with gold and jewels and pearls, holding in her hand a golden cup full of abominations and the impurities of her fornication; and on her forehead was written a name, a mystery: "Babylon the great, mother of whores and of earth's abominations. And I saw that the woman was drunk with the blood of the witnesses to Jesus. When I saw her, I was greatly amazed. But the angel said to me, "Why are you so amazed? I will tell you the mystery of the woman, and of the beast with seven heads and ten horns that carries her. The beast that you saw was, and is not, and is about to ascend from the bottomless pit and go to destruction. And the inhabitants of the earth, whose names have not been written in the book of life from the foundation of the world, will be amazed when they see the beast, because it was and is not and is to come. "This calls for a mind that has wisdom: the seven heads are seven mountains on which the woman is seated; also, they are seven kings, of whom five have fallen, one is living, and the other has not yet come; and when he comes, he must remain only a little while. As for the beast that was and is not, it is an eighth but it belongs to the seven, and it goes to destruction. And the ten horns that you saw are ten kings who have not yet received a kingdom, but they are to receive a kingdom, but they are to receive authority as kings for one hour, together with the beast. These are united in yielding their power and authority to the beast; they will make war on the Lamb, and the Lamb will conquer them, for he is Lord of lords and King of kings, and those with him are called and chosen and faithful." And he said to me, "The water that you saw, where the whore is seated, are peoples and multitudes and nations and languages. And the ten horns that you saw, they and the beast will hate the whore; they will make her desolate and naked; they will devour her flesh and burn her up with fire. For God has put it into their hearts to carry out his purpose by agreeing to give their kingdom to the beast, until the words of God will be fulfilled. The woman you saw is the great city that rules over the kings of the earth."

And the kings of the earth, who committed fornication and lived in luxury with her, will weep and wail over her when they see the smoke of her burning; they will stand far off, in fear of her torment, and say,

> "Alas, alas, the great city,
> Babylon, the mighty city!
> For in one hour your judgment has come."

And the merchants of the earth weep and mourn for her, since no one buys their cargo anymore, cargo of gold, silver, jewels and pearls, fine linen, purple, silk and scarlet, all kinds of scented wood, all articles of ivory, all articles of costly wood, bronze, iron, and marble, cinnamon, spice, incense, myrrh, frankincense, wine, olive oil, choice flour and wheat, cattle and sheep, horses and chariots, slaves—and human lives.

> "The fruit for which your soul longed
> has gone from you,
> and all your dainties and your splendor
> are lost to you,
> never to be found again!"

The merchants of these wares, who gained wealth from her, will stand far off, in fear of her torment, weeping and mourning aloud,

> "Alas, Alas, the great city,
> clothed in fine linen, in purple and scarlet,
> adorned with gold, with jewels, and with pearls!
> For in one hour all this wealth has been laid waste!"

Group 4: The Bride—Revelation 19:7–8; 21:1–4; 22:17

> Let us rejoice and exult
> and give him the glory,
> for the marriage of the Lamb has come,
> and his bride has made herself ready;
> to her it has been granted to be clothed
> with fine linen, bright and pure"—
> for the fine linen is the righteous deeds of the saints.

Then I saw a new heaven and a new earth; for the first heaven and the first earth had passed away, and the sea was no more. And I saw the holy city, the new Jerusalem, coming down out of heaven from God, prepared as a bride adorned for her husband. And I heard a loud voice from the throne saying,

"See, the home of God is among mortals.
He will dwell with them as their God;
they will be his peoples,
and God himself will be with them;
he will wipe every tear from heir eyes.
Death will be no more;
mourning and crying and pain will be no more,
for the first things have passed away."

The Spirit and the bride say, "Come."
And let everyone who hears say, "Come."
And let everyone who is thirsty come.
Let anyone who wishes take the water of life as a gift.

QUESTIONS FOR DISCUSSION AND/OR INDIVIDUAL REFLECTION

Use the following questions to look into each woman image/metaphor:

1. Describe the characteristics of the image. What role does it convey in the narrative text? What are the strengths and weaknesses?

2. Is there any injustice or act of violence that has been committed against the image? Relate the situation to experiences of women today or to yourself.

3. Which characteristics of the image you have explored should women seek to emulate or not to emulate? To which of these characteristics are you particularly drawn? Why?

Sharing and Reflection

Ask a group presenter to share with the rest of the participants some highlights from their text exploration. (Individual readers: Reflect on your exploration.)

Contextualization

Ask the participants to return to their previous groupings. Give each group a large sheet of newsprint, crayons, coloring pens, and thumbtacks or masking tape. Have them draw symbols showing images of an "ideal woman" on the newsprint and then display the sheets on the wall. Ask a group presenter to explain the symbols.

Responding in Faith

Name a concrete response of solidarity you can contribute in supporting women's issues. Write it on a piece of paper. In a group setting, read it at closing worship.

A Moment of Reflection

AFFIRMATION OF HOPE
(to be read privately or corporately)

Women's Creed

We (I) believe in the goodness and value of women; our (my) strength and sanity; our (my) willingness to weep; our (my) capacity to support each other, instead of being rivals; our (my) ability to cope with children's demands and the burdens of life; our (my) willingness and ability to get on with the job; our (my) spirituality; and our (my) earthiness, flowing with life, birth, and death.

We (I) affirm the story of women as the story of humankind: food gatherers and farmers; child-rearers and teachers; pioneers and policy-makers; needleworkers and textile-makers; homemakers and factory workers; parents, scientists, doctors; housekeepers and economists; givers of life; creators of arts and thoughts; unpaid hidden workers at home and paid members of the workforce outside. We (I) rejoice in our (my) diversity and versatility, our (my) intuition and our (my) logic.

We (I) confess our (my) failures, frailties, and imperfections, including our (my) past acceptance of violence and injustice in relationships between women and men. We (I) look forward to the future in faith and hope, working for the day when we (I) and all our (my) sisters no longer have to fit a stereotype, but are free to use all our gifts and to share in all the benefits of human life and work.

We (I) look forward to the age of peace, when violence is banished; both women and men are able to love and to be loved, and the work and wealth of our world is justly shared.

We (I) believe that our (my) future depends on us (me), but that all the forces for good, love, peace, and justice, all the creative powers of the universe work with all humankind to achieve that vision.

May it come soon. . . . Amen.[1]

Song of Inspiration

"Be Near Me, O God" (words and music: Colleen Fulmer, 1984) or

"Spirit of God Descend upon My Heart" (words: George Croly, 1854; music: Frederick C. Atkinson, 1870) *or*

"Be Thou My Vision" (words: 8th century Irish song; trans. Mary Elizabeth Byrne, 1905; vers. Eleanor H. Hull, 1912; music: traditional Irish melody)

Sharing of Commitment

Each participant may read his or her written response in solidarity with women. (Individual readers: Reflect on your written response.)

CLOSING PRAYER

May God, our empowerer, encourage us to go forth in a journey of "persistent resistance." May Jesus be our inspiration in bringing about women's empowerment. May the Holy Spirit create in us a vision of love, justice and peace. This day and in the days to come. Amen!

Session Assessment

Evaluate your learnings and/or discernments.

Session 2

Prophetic Voices of Women

Revelation 2:18-24

"And to the angel of the church in Thyatira write: Theses are the words of the Son of God, who has eyes like a flame of fire, and whose feet are like burnished bronze:

"I know your works—your love, faith, service, and patient endurance. I know that your last works are greater than the first. But I have this against you: you tolerate that woman Jezebel, who calls herself a prophet and is teaching and beguiling my servants to practice fornication and to eat food sacrificed to idols. I gave her time to repent, but she refuses to repent of her fornication. Beware, I am throwing her on a bed, and those who commit adultery with her I am throwing into great distress, unless they repent of her doings; and I will strike her children dead. And all the churches will know that I am the one who searches minds and hearts, and I will give to each of you as your works deserve.

Objectives

❧ To explore different avenues of women's prophetic voices for their self-worth and liberation.

❧ To become familiar with women prophets in the Bible.

❧ To study the life of the prophetess "Jezebel" and her contributions to church and society.

Community Circle or Individual Centering

OPENING SONG

"Here I Am, Lord" (words and music: Daniel L. Schutte, S.J., 1981) *or*

"We Have This Ministry" (words and music: Jim Strathdee, 1979) *or*

"Spirit, Spirit of Gentleness" (words and music: James K. Manley, 1979)

OPENING PRAYER

We (I) are created in your image, Mother, sister, friend:
creative life-givers,
strong and interdependent,
vital parts of sustaining networks of relationship and community.
We (I) have in us the seeds of likeness to you:
your love that flows to all,
your strong gentleness,
your wisdom and humour,
your compassion and desire for justice.
In the freedom of your friendship and sustaining love,
we (I) hope to find ourselves (myself) and liberation.
Liberation from the ways we (I) have been labelled or limited,
and the freedom to understand and love ourselves (myself).
Thank you, loving God. Amen.[1]

OPENING UP

Divide the participants into two groups. Assign one group to read a summary on the life of the prophet Huldah (2 Kings 22–23) and the other group to read about the life of the prophetic daughters of Philip (Acts 21:8–14). (Individual readers: Select a reading on the life of Huldah or the prophetic daughters of Philip.)

Group I: Huldah, The Female Prophet (2 Kings 22-23)

Female prophets in the Hebrew Scriptures were not very popular, but according to historical accounts, there are evidences of their existence in Mari and Assyria. However, it is very hard to determine from this isolated case the roles or frequency of female prophets in Judah. These prophets, like their male counterparts, expressed oracles and prophecies, some of which were addressed to kings on matters of safety and divine protection.[2]

During the reign of King Josiah in Judah, there was a female prophet named Huldah. She was the wife of Shallum, "keeper of the wardrobe." Huldah is the only female prophet mentioned in the book of Kings. She is alternately identified as a cult or court prophet. However, from the role she played in 2 Kings, she is more likely a court prophet.[3]

According to the narrative, Huldah's prophetic pronouncements are divided into two parts. The first part is a word of judgment against Judah. She prophesied that catastrophic disaster would strike the nation, but King Josiah would be spared because he was a penitent, humble man. The second is a word of assurance to the king that he would die in peace before that judgment was carried out. Only half of her prophecy came true. The second part of the oracle is not fulfilled. Josiah did not die in peace but in war.

The turning point of Huldah's prophetic role is seen when Josiah sent his officers to seek Huldah's counsel concerning the book of the Mosaic law that had been found during the temple repair. It can be noted here that it was after receiving Huldah's advice that Josiah carried out his religious reforms.

This significant historical role that Huldah played has both inspired and puzzled subsequent leaders of synagogues and churches. Several male prophets lived nearby during her time: Jeremiah, Zephaniah, and Nahum. All of them assisted Josiah in his effort to eradicate the Assyrian religion and return to the best Israelite traditions. Despite the availability of those able prophets, however, it was only Huldah who was able to interpret the book of law that made King Josiah successful in his project. Modern readers are amazed that a king and his male delegation would seek expert knowledge from a woman. What Huldah, the female prophet, declared to be of unique importance, we now call the "core of the Book of Deuteronomy."[4]

Group 2: Philip's Prophetic Daughters (Acts 21:8-14)

Philip the Evangelist, one of the seven apostles chosen in Jerusalem to assist in ministry, had four daughters endowed with the gift of prophecy. They are acknowledged by Eusebius, the historian, as women prophets and transmitters of apostolic tradition who were very famous in Asia. The author of Acts says nothing about the women, yet Eusebius would tell of their fame, noting their influence in other places and their prophetic powers. They are evidences that the gift of prophecy was the privilege of women in the early church, though they weren't given proper recognition.

The sisters, who never married, lived with their father in Caesarea on the Palestinian coast. They settled there after leaving Jerusalem when Stephen was stoned. It was contrary to their culture that all four were unmarried. In the context of prophetic utterances, they remained strangely silent.

In the book of Acts, the disciples at Tyre, speaking in the Spirit, begged Paul not to go to Jerusalem for it was too dangerous to do so. At Philip's house, a Judean prophet arrived and repeated the same warning with graphic detail. Did the daughters also speak but were ignored?

Prophetic leadership was common in the Pauline community and women prophesied in the churches. Paul wrote extensively about this phenomenon in his first letter to the church at Corinth (1 Cor. 11–14). This is also a manifestation that the practice of prophecy in the Hebrew scriptures was again alive.

As accounted for by Eusebius, these four female prophets demonstrate the fulfillment of Joel's prophecy: Then afterward, (God speaking): "I will pour out my spirit on all flesh; your sons and your daughters shall prophesy, and your old men shall dream dreams, and your young men shall see visions." (Joel 2:28 RSV). [5]

Group Discussion and/or Individual Reflection

What particular prophetic role or function did the female prophets play in each narrative?

What prophetic messages did they relay to their societies?

What is the significance of their message for the church today?

From the narratives explored, how do you define what a female prophet is?

Biblical Text Exploration

Read: Revelation 2:18-24

Background: Jezebel and the Church at Thyatira

The city of Thyatira was founded by the Lydian kingdom and later captured by Seleucus, a brave general of Alexander the Great. The city, having no natural defenses, was subject to repeated invasions. Its strengths lay largely in its strategic location and the very rich and fertile area surrounding it. Thyatira's inhabitants were descendants of Macedonian soldiers and retained much of their ancestors' militancy.[6]

In 189 B.C.E., Rome defeated Antiochus and the city of Thyatira was amalgamated with the kingdom of Pergamum and became a Roman ally. Prosperity attracted many Jewish people to come and reside in the area. The most common commercial trades of the city were the manufacturing of textiles and bronze armor.[7]

In the message to the church in Thyatira, John (the writer) commended the members for their love, faith, service, and endurance. But the influence of paganism is still reflected in their lifestyle. John conveyed his sharp disapproval to those members and followers who tolerated the teachings of the female prophet "Jezebel," considered to be the leader.[8]

John opposes Jezebel, which implies that she was a rival to his prophetic followings. Two devices were used to discredit her as a false prophet. First, he calls her "Jezebel," which connects her with the ill-famed woman who opposed Elijah and supported the prophets of Baal (1 Kings 16:31; 19:1–3). Second, John quoted Christ in a traditional language for a charge of false prophecy when Christ accuses Jezebel of "teaching and beguiling my servants to practice fornication and to eat food sacrificed to idols" (Rev. 2:20).[9]

What is the controversy?

In early Christianity, there was a fierce debate about whether Christians should eat the meat left over from sacrifices made to idols. Much of the meat available for consumption in the marketplace, public festivals, and private gatherings would have been considered as "sacrificial meat." Some members of the church at Thyatira, known as "Nicolaitans," with whom "Jezebel" may have been connected, were said to be advocates of eating sacrificial meat and practicing "fornication." This practice offered political, economic, and professional advantages to Christians living in the city. The meat sacrificed to idols was served at meetings of trade guilds and business associations as well as at private receptions. It allowed the Christians to participate actively in the commercial, political, and social life of the city.[10]

Read the text again and, this time, assume that the class setting is in the church at Thyatira in the first century.

QUESTIONS FOR DISCUSSION AND/OR INDIVIDUAL REFLECTION

1. What are the strengths and weaknesses of the church at Thyatira?

2. What does the symbolic name "Jezebel" reveal about the woman in this church? What are the grounds in condemning her? Do you agree with them?

3. Would "Jezebel" really have remained silent in such a spirit-charged setting right in her own church? Who has played a role similar to "Jezebel" in your life? Share this experience with the group.

Contextualization

Read the following text changing Jezebel into a male prophet who was condemned by John for political idolatry or fornication. How would you react? Do you feel the same as when it was a woman?

Male-Image Text: Revelation 2:18-24

Verse 18—And to the angel of the church in Thyatira write: These are the words of the Son of God, who has eyes like a flame of fire, and whose feet are like burnished bronze:

Verse 19—I know your works—your love, faith, service, and patient endurance. I know that your last works are greater than the first.

Verse 20—But I have this against you: you tolerate that man "Jezebel," who calls himself a prophet and is teaching and beguiling my servants to practice fornication and to eat food sacrificed to idols.

Verse 21—I gave him time to repent, but he refuses to repent of his fornication.

Verse 22—Beware, I am throwing him on a bed, and those who commit adultery with him I am throwing into great distress, unless they repent of his doings;

Verse 23—and I will strike his children dead. And all the churches will know that I am the one who searches minds and hearts, and I will give to each of you as your works deserve.

Verse 24—But to the rest of you at Thyatira, who do not hold this teaching, who have not learned what some call "the deep things of Satan," to you I say, I do not lay on you any other burden.

Name some women whose lifestyles can be compared with Jezebel. Cite some issues or root causes that challenged these women to prophesy or to "voice out" their grievances and assert their options, prerogatives or choices in a system not welcomed by some church people.

Responding in Faith

Complete each phrase to form a sentence that affirms prophetic voices of women:

If I were a prophet, my role would be . . .

To speak like a prophet is to . . .

Jezebel is labeled as a bad prophet by John. I see her as . . .

Share these affirmations with the group.
(Individual readers: Write sentences in a journal.)

A Moment of Reflection

Song

"A Prophet-Woman Broke a Jar" (words: Brian Wren, 1991; music: Walter K. Stanton, 1951) *or*

"Day of Justice" (words and music: Miriam Therese Winter, 1982)

Responsive Reading

Psalm of Prophetic Ministry

Leader: Thus says Shaddai: my daughters, prophesy!

All: What shall we prophesy?

Leader: Prophesy on love.

All: On that day, we will feel and know the fullness of love within us, for women will come together in a love that spirals outward to embrace a global sisterhood whose love will welcome all.

Leader: Thus says Shekinah: my daughters, prophesy!

All: What shall we prophesy?

Leader: Prophesy on presence.

All: On that day, no walls will keep one person from another, and two inone flesh will pale before the mystery of two in one soul and spirit, as women, fully present, herald the presence of God.

Leader: Thus says Sophia: my daughters, prophesy!

All: What shall we prophesy?

Leader: Prophesy on wisdom.

All: On that day, the wise will know the questions to the answers, as women make sense of all the myths from the dream time of creation until the moment after now, spinning a single story from diverse apocrypha.

Leader: Thus says the Spirit: my daughters, prophesy!

All: How can we prophesy?

Leader: Prophesy in the Spirit.

All: On that day, all flesh will proclaim the good news of salvation, women speak their inner truth; daughters, sisters, mothers, wives; and pray for this gift of freedom for the men who share their lives.[11]

CLOSING PRAYER

Lord, Shaddai,* we (I) give you thanks for your female power within us (me), for courage to speak your secret word, grace to put it into practice, strength to endure the ridicule and the pressure of constraint. Be with us (me) now and always as we (I) settle ourselves (myself) within You, and visit with grace the ones we (I) love. This is the prayer we (I) pray. Amen.[12]

Session Assessment

Evaluate your learnings and/or discernments.

---

*Shaddai—A Hebrew word for God which could mean almighty, all-powerful, or God of High Places.

Session 3

The Struggles of Giving Birth

Revelation 12:1-6

A great portent appeared in heaven: a woman clothed with the sun, with the moon under her feet, and on her head a crown of twelve stars. She was pregnant and was crying out in birthpangs, in the agony of giving birth. Then another portent appeared in heaven: a great red dragon, with seven heads and ten horns, and seven diadems on his heads. His tail swept down a third of the stars of heaven and threw them to the earth. Then the dragon stood before the woman who was about to bear a child, so that he might devour her child as soon as it was born. And she gave birth to a son, a male child, who is to rule all the nations with a rod of iron. But her child was snatched away and taken to God and to his throne: and the woman fled into the wilderness, where she has a place prepared by God, so that there she can be nourished for one thousand two hundred sixty days.

Objectives

❧ To discover what women's struggles are expressed in the text and to discuss their implications for the current conditions of women.

❧ To identify the root causes of women's disempowerment and cite ways for their empowerment.

❧ To acknowledge the different "motherly" qualities of God as points of reflection for today's women.

Community Circle or Individual Centering

OPENING SONG

"Rahamin, Compassion" (words and music: Colleen Fulmer, 1985) *or*

"Dear Mother God" (words: Janet Wootton; music: R. R. Terry, 1933) *or*

"Mother and God" (words and music: Miriam Therese Winter, 1987; arr. Nan Thompson, 1995)

After singing one of the suggested songs together once, share with the group a word or phrase describing God's motherly attributes. Sing the song once more and liven things up with hand clapping and other percussion.

OPENING PRAYER

Birthing, life-giving God
you have nourished us (me) with your life-giving breast
and you taught us (me) how to struggle against the dragons of our time.
Bless us (me) as we (I) gather to bring new visions for the world.
Fill us (me) with your creative wisdom as we (I) give birth
to a new heaven and a new earth.
Amen.

OPENING UP

Ask each participant to select his or her own group of interest. (Individual readers: Write responses in a journal or on a pad.)

Group 1: Picture Analysis

Task: Show some pictures of women giving birth. Discuss what it is like to give birth (the labor pains, the joy of cuddling the newborn, feeding the baby, etc.).

Group 2: Experience in Birth-Giving

Task: Comment on this perspective: "Birth-giving is a form of struggle between life and death." Analyze and discuss.

Group 3: Mothers-to-Be

Task: If you were to become a mother, how would you raise your child?

Biblical Text Exploration

Read: Revelation 12:1-6

Background

In this text, John's symbolism fuses images from the Hebrew Scriptures with images from ancient myths about the births of certain gods and about divine combat with monsters of chaos.[1]

Elisabeth Schüssler Fiorenza contends that the myth of the queen of heaven with the divine child was internationally known at the time of John. Variations of this story appear in Babylonia, Egypt, Greece, Asia Minor, and especially in the text about astral religion. Elements of this myth are: the goddess and the divine child; the great red dragon and his enmity to mother and child; and the motif of the protection of the mother and child. Some features of this international myth appear also in the Roman imperial cult. A coin in Pergamum, for instance, shows the goddess Roma with the divine emperor. In the cities of Asia Minor, Roma, the Queen of Heaven, was worshiped as the mother of the gods. Her oldest temple stood in Smyrna. Her imperial child, Apollo, was celebrated as the world's savior. It is possible that John connects such metaphor to the imperial cult and the goddess Roma insofar as he pictures the woman clothed with the sun as the anti-image of Babylon, the symbol of the world power of his days and his allies.[2] The "woman" is often interpreted as the figure of Israel, the historical mother of Jesus, the church, or the messianic community under persecution. She can also be seen as the whole cosmos groaning in pain.[3]

The woman's celestial motif (sun, moon, and the stars) associates her with a high goddess, "a queen of heaven." Several pagan goddesses such as Artemis (Ephesus), Atargatis (Syria), and Isis (Egypt) were all linked with stars and planets in ancient mythology.[4]

John reinterprets this international ancient myth in terms of Jewish expectations. His emphasis on the plight of the woman was inspired by the Hebrew Scriptures' image of Israel-Zion in messianic times. The vision of the woman in labor pain alludes to Israel-Zion, seen in Isaiah (26:16–17; 54:1; 66:7–9) as a mother awaiting the delivery of the messianic age (Mic. 4:9–10). John invokes the image of the messianic child being born accompanied by the birth pangs of the messianic woes. This child represents without question Jesus Christ, who is exalted and receives the powers of messianic kingship.

The figure of the dragon is also familiar to ancient mythology. In Jewish writings, it frequently serves as a symbol of an oppressor nation such as Egypt (Ps. 74:14) and its ruler, Pharaoh (Ezek. 32:2ff), or Syria and Babylon (Isa. 27:1). Daniel uses this symbol for the last great antidivine nation and its ruler, the opponent of Israel. Within this context, readers can understand the red dragon as the ultimate foe of the people of God.[5]

QUESTIONS FOR DISCUSSION AND/OR INDIVIDUAL REFLECTION

Ask one participant to read the text dramatically. (Individual readers: Read the text aloud.)

Discuss the following questions. (Individual readers: Write in a journal or on a pad.)

1. Describe the woman, the dragon, and the child. In your opinion, what does each one represent?

2. What is the significance of the woman's crying in pain and anguish?

3. Why did the woman flee into the wilderness or to a place prepared for her by God?

4. Was it fair for the woman to have her child snatched away and taken to God? Why or why not? What does this gesture symbolize?

Contextualization

In today's context, what conditions suppress women's rights to nurture or care for their children? Cite some current issues that affect women in this regard.

Responding in Faith

MEDITATION
Woman Clothed with the Sun

We have known the dragon. He is apartheid and war, hunger and sexual violence, poverty and patriarchy. He is all that lurks nearby, ready to devour that which we long to bring to birth. He is the enemy of justice and compassion and community, the destroyer of peace.

Revelation offers us a beautiful portrait of a woman empowered. She is clothed in sun, upheld by the moon, crowned with stars, swathed in the power of Creator and creation. Her womb is brimming with life, vibrant with possibility. The world is hers.

The waves of pain begin—the agonizing end that ushers in a bold beginning. She weeps, cries out, holds on, lets go, submits to a force of life beyond herself. And all the while the dragon waits; a monster so large his tail can take out a third of the stars in one swipe. He stands there, by her side, jaws open and ready to devour the thing she loves most.

Her son is to rule by the power of justice. But he is snatched away—not by the dragon but by the bearers of children to God. He is safe, and so is the woman. In the wilderness, far from all that is comfortable and known, there is a place for her. Nourishment waits. She can rest.

But the dragon is not through. He pursues the woman. And this time, she is given the wings of an eagle to soar away and back to the wilderness to her place, to be nourished for "a time and times, and half a time." She can stay as long as she likes.

This woman is considered by some to be a symbol of Mary or of the church. She reflects each of us as well. We all know the joyful agony of giving birth to something, whatever it is we are bringing to life, whatever our longing and labor. The monsters lurk, threatening to devour our creativity, our confidence, our life.

But the monsters do not win. The dragon loses in the end, while the woman soars in glorious freedom on eagle's wings. The creativity and compassion of God cannot be stopped. The woman cannot be subdued.

The woman's son will rule, but it is she who is robed in glorious splendor, she who stands face to face with the dragon, she for whom God has prepared a place. It looks like a wilderness, but it is a place of rest and nourishment. In the most desolate places, God nurtures and provides.

She is a woman of power. If she were not, the dragon would not have bothered. But he persists. Her power is a threat to all that he stands for. But her trust in a God of light and love saves and sustains her. God bears her up on wings. A dance that God began with Eve continues through time. God and the woman soar like one being.

God dances still. The spirit is in the wings, and we are all invited to soar; for each one of us is clothed with the sun, bearing glory and honor created in the image of God.[6]

Think of a woman who needs your concern at this particular moment. In silence, offer a prayer for her.

A Moment of Reflection

SONG

"El Shaddai" (words and music: Colleen Fulmer, 1985) *or*

"Mothering God You Gave Me Birth" (words: Julian of Norwich, 1400; adapt. Jean Wiebe Jurzen, 1991; music: Henry Baker, 1854)

RESPONSIVE REFLECTION

The Struggles of Bringing to Birth

Leader: Our universe is precious and vulnerable as a pregnant woman. The earth and its people are crying out in birth pangs in anguish and in pain.

People: The agony of birth-giving is not like the pains of battlefields and wounds and dead corpses. The pains of giving birth to a new creation contain the joy of newness in hope. Our struggle is a struggle in hope of new life.

Leader: The earth and its people are giving birth in front of beasts and dragons who wish to devour newness and change and who threaten and are threatened by the millions of little children.

People: The woman struggling in giving birth invites all of us to give birth to newness in front of the dragon, trusting God who will protect the new creation and ourselves.

All: The new creation has begun with Jesus Christ. As followers of Jesus Christ, and as God's new creation, we must continue to witness to the power of love and to decry and name the dragons of our time. Let us join the labor pains in solidarity with women and men in their struggle for justice. Amen.[7]

CLOSING PRAYER

O One who brings to birth in us, who has midwifed all creation, who has power to open the womb of blessing and to close the womb of strife, give us the means of bringing to birth the world we are awaiting, and strength to stay the course. We believe that what we set out to accomplish will one day come to pass in you and through you, Creator of all, and Midwife of the Living. Praise be to You, Shaddai. Amen.[8]

Session Assessment

Evaluate your learnings and/or discernments.

Session 4

Women Say NO! to War

Revelation 12:7-17

And war broke out in heaven: Michael and his angels fought against the dragon. The dragon and his angels fought back, but they were defeated, and there was no longer any place for them in heaven. The great dragon was thrown down, that ancient serpent, who is called the Devil and Satan, the deceiver of the whole world—he was thrown down to the earth, and his angels were thrown down with him. Then I heard a loud voice in heaven, proclaiming,

> *"Now have come the salvation and the power*
> > *and the kingdom of our God*
> > *and the authority of his Messiah,*
> *for the accuser of our comrades has been thrown down,*
> > *who accuses them day and night before our God.*
> *But they have conquered him by the blood of the Lamb*
> > *and by the word of their testimony,*
> *for they did not cling to life even in the face of death.*
> *Rejoice then, you heavens*
> > *and those who dwell in them!*
> *But woe to the earth and the sea,*
> > *for the devil has come down to you*
> *with great wrath,*
> > *because he knows that his time is short!"*

So when the dragon saw that he had been thrown down to the earth, he pursued the woman who had given birth to the male child. But the woman was given the two wings of the great eagle, so that she could fly from the serpent into the wilderness, to her place where she is nourished for a time, and times, and half a time. Then from his mouth the serpent poured water like a river after the woman, to sweep her away with the flood. But the earth came to the help of the woman; it opened its mouth and swallowed the river that the dragon had poured from his mouth. Then the dragon was angry with the woman, and went off to make war on the rest of her children, those who keep the commandments of God and hold the testimony of Jesus.

Objectives

❧ To define the meaning and causes of war and its effects on women.

❧ To trace several war stories of our times and be able to relate them to the "war" depicted in the text.

❧ To create slogans or posters denouncing war and its destructive effects on the whole of creation.

Community Circle or Individual Centering

OPENING SONG

"Cry of Ramah" (words and music: Colleen Fulmer, 1985) *or*

"When Quiet Peace Is Shattered" (words: St Francis of Assisi; music: Sebastian Temple, 1967) *or*

"Let There Be Peace on Earth" (words and music: Sy Miller and Jill Jackson, 1955)

OPENING PRAYER

Peace-loving God, we (I) are (am) surrounded by hatred and violence,
of wars that torment people of all ages, especially women and children.
May you challenge us (me) to be peacekeepers and peacemakers,
so that we (I) can make a difference in the world.

Surround us (me) with a hope that heals the broken, violent,
  tormented world.
In the name of Jesus, who brings us peace. Amen.

OPENING UP

Group the participants in pairs. Give each pair a set of pictures depicting wars in different times and settings. Let each pair discuss the questions. (Individual readers: Have pictures of war available for viewing. Reflect on the questions.)

1. What do these pictures suggest about war?

2. Describe its effects on the whole of creation. Do you think war is necessary to the peacemaking process? Why or why not?

Share your pictures and reflections with the group. Create some dance steps to the song "Cry of Ramah" or another similar song.

Biblical Text Exploration

Read: Revelation 12:7-17

BACKGROUND

Women and War

The apocalypse of women has always included the horrors of war. What does it mean for women to read the ultimate war narrative? Is this violent version of the end of time the story women want to tell? the story women want to be involved in?

Revelation describes the final eschatological battle in all its extreme violence and gory detail. This war is "The war to end all wars." God's army conquers the evil powers. The believers who are called to "patient endurance" must resist nonviolently, but this resistance is active, not passive, since the result of being a witness might be death. What are women's roles in this war? How are contemporary women readers to respond to God's war?

The violence and vengeance in Revelation come out of persecution, both real and perceived, that was experienced by Christians in the Roman Empire at the end of the first century. The violence of the book is startling: violence is done to nature, people, and supernatural beings. There are swords and slaughter, hunger and martyrs.

The war is bloody. There are casualties on both sides. Cannibalism is part of the warfare tactics (Rev. 19:17–18). There is torture in the lake of fire and sulfur (Rev. 20:10). All the enemies and every impure thing is destroyed. The new Jerusalem comes down to replace the old city (Rev. 21:1–2). There is no evil or pollution in the new world. The new world of God surpasses the old Roman world.

Women's response to the coming apocalypse has to be a reinterpretation of what it means to choose Christ over Caesar. Choosing Christ no longer means desiring martyrdom. When two-thirds of the earth's population goes to bed hungry each night, martyrdom becomes another form of patriarchal abuse. Christ is more than a sacrificial lamb who resurrected into a mythic warrior hero. Women have to refuse the call to mimic such sacrifice. Women (and men!) must be involved in risk-taking for social change.

Revelation ends after the war, after the destruction of the old earth. A "utopia" is set up by God. "Death will be no more; mourning and crying and pain will be no more, for the first things have passed away" (Rev. 21:4). God and the Lamb dwell inside the city with the chosen people. The new world is perfectly pure, and there is no more suffering.[1]

TEXT INTERPRETATION
Revelation 12:7-12

This text reveals the deepest cause for the persecution and oppression experienced by Christians in the time of John. Its mythological symbolization of the "war in heaven" serves to explain, in the language of the Jewish myth, the role of Satan or the Devil. In this tradition, Yahweh, the divine warrior, waged battles on behalf of the Israelites. The holy war traditions portrayed Israel's enemies symbolically as dragonlike monsters (Isa. 27:1; 51:9). The "dragon" in Revelation 12 represents both the political and cosmic enemies of the church. It also symbolizes the powers of the Roman Empire, which promoted idolatry through social and political means. John's symbolism suggests that God will defeat the church's earthly adversaries, just as God's servant Michael had defeated the heavenly adversary.

The description of the woman's flight to the "wilderness" on "two wings of the great eagle" recalls God's rescue of the Hebrew children from Egypt and Pharaoh on "eagle's wings" (Exod. 19:4; Deut. 32:11; Isa. 40:31). This must have helped the first century believers interpret their own social and historical situation in a similar context. They would have perceived that they were the rest of the woman's offspring and so still under siege by the dragon.[2]

OTHER SYMBOLIC INTERPRETATIONS

1.   Michael, an angel whose name means "who is like God," stands as the leader of God's army. He is mentioned three times in the book of Daniel as "one of the chief princes" (Dan. 10:13), "your prince" (10:21) and "the great prince" (12:1). He is called the "archangel" who contended with the devil over the body of Moses (Jude 9), and possibly is the archangel mentioned in 1 Thessalonians 4:16.

2.   The dragon or serpent is seen as the opponent of God (evil), identifying him with the serpent in Eden (Genesis 3) through whom sin was introduced into the world.

3.   The phrase, "a time, and times and half a time" (Rev. 12:14) is equivalent to the twelve hundred sixty days of Revelation 12:6 (the period during which God nourished the Israelites in the wilderness). Although the wilderness is a place of withdrawal where God's people are protected and nurtured, it is also a place where the struggle is great.

4.   The idea of floods threatening to engulf God's people was not new; it is found repeatedly in the prophets and psalms. The water that tried to engulf the woman out of the dragon's mouth can be interpreted as anything that defiles God: delusions and lies, false impressions of invincible power, destruction, oppression,

indifference and discrimination, poverty and hunger, and so on.

5. The earth opening its mouth can be interpreted as God's grace and power that saved the "woman" from the destructive forces of the dragon.

6. The war to some interpreters is a spiritual war between God and the devil; to others, this is the war between good and evil. In contemporary times, this is a clash between the powerful (the rich) and the powerless (the poor).[3]

QUESTIONS FOR DISCUSSION AND/OR INDIVIDUAL REFLECTION

Recap the text from the previous session, Revelation 12:1–6. Ask a participant to read the new text, Revelation 12:7–17. Then analyze the text with these questions.

1. Verses 7–8. Describe the war. What kind of war was portrayed? Who were the opponents?

2. Verse 9. What happened to the dragon? What does this signify?

3. Verses 10–12. Who do you think John is referring to as the speaker in these particular verses? What was the message?

4. Verses 13–14. The dragon couldn't easily give up! What did he do? What does the gesture of giving the woman "two wings of the great eagle" symbolize? What happened afterwards?

5. Verses 15–17. What is the significance of the earth "opening its mouth and swallowing the river" that the dragon poured from its mouth? Do you believe that the dragon still exists in our present time? In what form(s)?

Contextualization

Discuss and/or reflect on the plight of women in East Timor by reading the following news report.

December 7, 1995 marks the twentieth anniversary of Indonesia's invasion of East Timor, an island country northwest of Australia. For twenty years Indonesia has illegally occupied East Timor, and so far over one-third of the population has been killed in what is now recognized as the worst genocide per capita since the Holocaust.

In East Timor today, women are forcibly sterilized as part of the Indonesian government's scheme to eliminate the Timorese. Families suspected of pro-independence activities are forced to have Indonesian soldiers live in their homes. East Timorese are not permitted to gather in groups of more than two, and all East Timorese must adhere to an 8 P.M. curfew. Study of East Timorese history, culture, and language is banned. Those who resist Indonesian rule risk torture, rape, murder, and disappearance.

Despite this oppression, the people of East Timor continue to actively resist and plan to demonstrate. A young Timorese woman who recently defected to Canada, and who is now living in Ottawa, explains that the youth in East Timor risk their lives by protesting, because they feel they will die anyway, and would rather die resisting. The slogan for these activists is "to resist is to win."[4]

What can we do as a group or as an individual to support the East Timorese in gaining back their freedom as a nation?

Responding in Faith

Make slogans or posters that denounce war. Examples:

MAKE PEACE NOT WAR!

WOMEN SAY NO TO WAR! SAVE THE WORLD!

WOMEN CAN MAKE A DIFERENCE! NO TO ARMS!

A Moment of Reflection
RECITE
(*in unison*)
Weep O My Sisters

Weep O my sisters, weep for the blood of women shed for you,
the blood of the matriarch, the blood of the prophetess, the
priestess, the revolutionary.
Weep for the women slaughtered, weep for the lovers raped,
weep for the daughters stolen, the mothers humbled and enslaved.
Weep until we rise in blood and flame to redress and rebirth![5]

SONGS OF PERSISTENT RESISTANCE

"She Flies On" (words and music: Gordon Light, 1985; arr.: Andrew
Donaldson, 1994) *or*

"O Day of Peace" (words: Carl P. Daw Jr., 1982; music: C. Hubert H.
Parry, 1916; arr.: Janet Wyatt, 1977)

MEMORIAL OFFERING

Offer the slogans and posters in memory of women who died in wars.

Sung Prayer: Rest In My Wings (an inspired Prayer of St. Teresa of Avila)

Don't be afraid, I'm holding you close in the darkness.
My love and my grace will carry you through the long night.
The love that I give bubbles in you like a fountain,
So rest in my wings and put all your fears to flight.

Though you be burdened, I will cradle you deep in my nest.
Though you be weary, my wings will enfold you in rest.
Though you be desert, my rivers will flow deep inside.
Though you be barren, I'll fill out your womb with new life.

Though you be orphaned, I'll always be here at your side.
Though you be empty, I'll bring forth new fruit on the vine.
Though you be thirsty, you'll drink from the well of my side.
Though you be hungry, the finest of bread I'll provide.[6]

BENEDICTION
(*in unison*)

Nothing should disturb you.
Nothing should frighten you.
Patience obtains everything.
If you have God, you lack nothing.
God alone suffices. Amen.[7]

Session Assessment

Evaluate your learnings and/or discernments.

Session 5

The Empowered Woman

Revelation 17:1-6

The woman was clothed in purple and scarlet, and adorned with gold and jewels and pearls, holding in her hand a golden cup full of abominations and the impurities of her fornication;

And I saw that the woman was drunk with the blood of the saints and the blood of the witnesses to Jesus. When I saw her, I was greatly amazed.

Objectives

♦ To discover the reasons why women have not fully realized their power.

♦ To discern how women's power is being used, abused or misused.

♦ To identify how women are empowered by God to become potential leaders in their own contexts.

Community Circle or Individual Centering

OPENING SONG

"Wings Unfurled" (words and music: Colleen Fulmer, 1989) *or*

"Spirit of Life" (words and music: Carolyn McDade, 1981; harm.: Grace Lewis-McLaren, 1992) *or*

"Maker of the Sun and Moon" (words and music: Peter Sharrocks, 1991; arr.: Simon Hester, 1991)

OPENING PRAYER

We (I) are (am) all women (a woman) of power.
Women of mystery and grace.
Remind us (me) to hold our (my) power lightly and use it wisely:
the power of loving service
the power of just compassion
the power of empathy and vulnerability.
We (I) are (am) all (a) women (woman) of power.
Women (Woman) of mystery and grace
Remind us (me) that we (I) are (am) made in your image
that we (I) too are (am a) creator(s) and creative
that you call us (me) to dance lightly with others and on our (my) planet
and to laugh! Amen.[1]

OPENING UP

The First Canadian Woman Judge

Emily Murphy, born Emily Ferguson, married an Anglican minister in 1887, at nineteen. At church, she organized activities and campaigns and voiced her concerns about social problems. Later, she began to write and speak out about the horrible side-effects of industrialization and ran a successful campaign to raise funds for the first hospital in Swan River, Manitoba.

In 1916, she became the first Canadian woman judge. Her first day, a lawyer objected to having his case heard by her, on the grounds that only men "could be persons in the statutes authorizing appointment of judges" (she overruled his objection and proceeded).

In 1927, Emily Murphy pleaded a case to the Supreme Court about whether women could be considered "persons." After a five-week debate, the Supreme Court ruled that women could not be considered "persons." However, the decision was appealed in England, and on

October 18, 1929, the Privy Council ruled that women were indeed "persons."

Throughout her lifetime, Judge Emily Murphy helped to divert thousands of women from crime and prostitution by helping them find employment and housing.[2]

QUESTIONS FOR REFLECTION

1. From the selection, what lessons on power have you learned?

2. Why do you think it was important to the Supreme Court of Canada that women not be considered persons?

3. How do you think Judge Murphy's actions have contributed to women's empowerment today?

Biblical Text Exploration

Read: Revelation 17:1-6
Background

After the third cycle of numbered visions, John reports that one of the seven angels showed him the judgment of the "great whore" who is seated on many waters, with whom kings of the earth have committed fornication (17:1–2a). She is decked out with purple, scarlet, and jewels, and she wears on her forehead a name, "a mystery": "Babylon the great, mother of whores and of earth's abominations" (17:5). The woman is seated on a "scarlet beast that was full of blasphemous names" (17:3).

The details of John's description indicate that the beast symbolizes the Roman Empire as a whole, while the woman represents the city of Rome (used as Babylon in the text). John's portrayal of the woman recalls the depiction of the goddess Roma on some ancient coins; she is seated on Rome's seven hills, with the river Tiber running below. Any Jew or Christian living in the last decades of the first century would have recognized that her "mysterious name" was a symbolic designation for Rome, which like the ancient Babylon, had conquered Jerusalem and destroyed the temple.[3]

John brings at least three charges against the city of Rome: (1) idolatry and sorcery, (2) violence, and (3) excessive wealth. Idolatry and sorcery are suggested both by the depiction of the city as a whore and by the proximity to the beast with "blasphemous names" (an allusion to the titles of honor given to emperors). The violence is seen in the passage, "[Babylon is] drunk with the blood of the saints and the blood of the witnesses to Jesus" (17:6). John seems to be deeply affected by the numerous persecutions of the Christians in Rome. Babylon's excessive wealth is tainted by the city's "fornication" (idolatry) and its acquisition has led to arrogance based on blasphemy.[4] Rome in its splendor, being carried and supported by the beast, must be understood as the magnificent symbol of imperial power and religion. Babylon is the powerful personification of international oppression and murder throughout the Roman Empire.[5]

John uses the image of woman to symbolize the present murderous reality of the imperial world power, as well as the life-nurturing reality of the renewed world of God. It must not be overlooked however, that such female imagery for cities utilizes conventional language. Then, as today, cities and countries were grammatically construed as feminine. The city was seen as a place of human culture and political institutions and does not tell us anything about the author's understanding of actual women.[6]

This text (Rev. 17:1–6), for Tina Pippin, is not liberating for women readers. She finds in Revelation only negative and male-dominated images of women. It ignores the gender roles and focuses on the political implications. She finds the violent destruction of Rome very cathartic, frightening, and horrifying and leading to a sense of hopelessness. This image became reality for women accused of witchcraft, a period of women's history Mary Daly refers to as "The Burning Times." Pippin cited: "The technological true believers of the Book of Revelation live their fatal faith, the faith of the Fathers. Knowing their own rightness or righteousness, they are participant observers in the stripping, eating, and burning of the "famous prostitute," the whore hated by God and the kings (leaders) (s)he has inspired. The "harlot" deserves to be hated and destroyed, of course, for she symbolizes the uncontrollable Babylon, the wicked city."[7]

Pippin now poses these questions to us: As women readers of Revelation, have we not been too willing participants in this scapegoating of the whore? Have we not accepted too readily the ideal image put before women by the patriarchy?[8]

QUESTIONS FOR DISCUSSION AND/OR INDIVIDUAL REFLECTION

1. What type of leadership does the woman (great whore) project in verses 1–2? *Insight:* Power can create "imperialism" in the name of diplomatic relationships.

2. How would you recognize that the woman was powerful? What can you say of her title and appearance? Can you justify her position in power (vv. 3–5)? *Insight:* Lust of power can be dangerous. It can make one a corrupt tyrant who is obsessed by every opportunity to manipulate and exploit people and systems.

3. What horrible acts did the woman commit against the saints and witnesses of Jesus Christ (v. 6)? What does this mean to you? *Insight:* Power is a worthy endeavor if exercised in a humanitarian way. On the other hand, it provides the temptation to dehumanize people.

4. John used the "whore" as a symbol for the cities of Rome or Babylon (superpowers in his time). By doing so, what damage did he do to the image of women? Is it irreparable? What steps can be taken to change this image?[9]

Contextualization

GROUP DISCUSSION AND/OR INDIVIDUAL EXPLORATION

1.   What is power? How do women differ from men in their exercise of power? In what ways are women powerful? Powerless?

2.   What are some problems that a female leader of the country might encounter? In what ways do you think her leadership would be tested? Do you think her struggles as a leader would be greater than her male counterparts? For what reasons?

3.   Can you think of a woman who has been verbally, psychologically, physically, or sexually abused? What could you do to make her "whole" again? How would God empower you in this situation?

Responding in Faith

Share the following with the group. (Individual readers: Write a word in a journal or on a pad.)

➤   A key word that represents to you what makes you powerless.

➤   A key word that empowers you.

A Moment of Reflection

RECITE
I Am a Woman

I believe that women are equal in ability to men; I believe that just because my mother accepted a subservient role, it does not mean I must, too. I believe that if I do not fight for the rights of my sister, then she will be oppressed. I believe that limitless horizons lie before my daughter, not just a few traditional choices; I believe that I have much to contribute to the world, and I alone possess my particular talents and abilities; I believe that each woman is an individual, not a stereotype. [10]

CLOSING SONG

"One by One" (words and music: Miriam Therese Winter, 1987) *or*

"God of Freedom, God of Justice" (words: Shirley Erena Murray, 1980; music: 17th century French traditional carol)

RESPONSIVE READING

A Psalm about Power

Voice 1: Women, what is power?

    All: Power is now power over. Power is not being overpowered.

Voice 2: Women, how do you exercise power?

    All: By taking control of ourselves. By refusing to be controlled by others.

Voice 3: Women, where do you get your power?

    All: From the One who is all-powerful. We name Her power! We claim Her power! Praise to Her who empowers us!

Voice 1: Women, what is power?

    All: Power is empowering. Power is not empiring.

Voice 2: Women, how do you exercise power?

    All: By empowering others to empower others. By creating empowering circles. By resisting empire-building.

Voice 3: Women, where do you get your power?

    All: From the One who is all-powerful. We name Her power! We claim Her power! Praise to Her who empowers us![11]

Empowerment Circle

In a circle, put your right hand on the shoulder of the one next to you and empower each other by saying these words: "(Name), may God's power be with you!"

Closing Prayer
(*in unison*)

Sacred Power, empowering all who are powerless and overpowered by all the forces rising up to take control of the universe by taking control of us, give us the means to change our status and forgive our triumphal traits, for we know that yours is the glory and power forever. Amen.[12]

Session Assessment

Evaluate your learnings and/or discernments.

Session 6

Becoming Whole Again!

Revelation 17:7-18

But the angel said to me, "Why are you so amazed? I will tell you the mystery of the woman, and of the beast with seven heads and ten horns that carries her. The beast that you saw was, and is not, and is about to ascend from the bottomless pit and go to destruction. And the inhabitants of the earth, whose names have not been written in the book of life from the foundation of the world, will be amazed when they see the beast, because it was and is not and is to come.

"This calls for a mind that has wisdom: the seven heads are seven mountains on which the woman is seated; also, they are seven kings, of whom five have fallen, one is living, and the other has not yet come; and when he comes, he must remain only a little while; As for the beast that was and is not, it is an eighth but it belongs to the seven, and it goes to destruction. And the ten horns that you saw are ten kings who have not yet received a kingdom, but they are to receive authority as kings for one hour, together with the beast. These are united in yielding their power and authority to the beast; they will make war on the Lamb, and the Lamb will conquer them, for he is Lord of lords and Kings of kings, and those with him are called and chosen and faithful."

And he said to me, "The waters that you saw, where the shore is seated, are peoples and multitudes and nations and languages. And the ten horns that you saw, they and the beast will hate the whore; they will make her desolate and naked; they will devour her flesh and burn her up with fire. For God has put it into there hearts to carry out his purpose by agreeing to give their kingdom to the beast, until the words of God will be fulfilled. The woman you saw is the great city that rules over the kings of the earth."

Objectives

♦ To discover what images are portrayed by the "prostitute" as discussed in the text.

♦ To understand the causes of women's prostitution in the biblical context as well as in our present times.

♦ To discern ways we can make to enable "prostituted women" to become whole again.

Community Circle or Individual Centering

OPENING SONG

"We Are the Body of Christ" (words: Martha Ann Kirk; music: Colleen Fulmer, 1985) *or*

"For the Healing of the Nations" (words: Fred Kaan, 1965; music: Henry Purcell, 1659–95) *or*

"Breathe on Me, Breath of God" (words: Edwin Hatch, 1878; music: Robert Jackson, 1888)

OPENING PRAYER

Undiscriminating God, some women are hurting
because of the unjust systems in our society
that violate their bodies and torment their spirits.
We (I) offer this time to think of our (my) sisters who are in this
condition,
that we may all unite and offer our support in prayers and solidarity.
Bless our bodies (my body), bless our spirits (my spirit),
make us (me) a vessel of your love and wisdom.
Heal our bodies (my body), heal our spirits (my spirit),
bring us (me) to compassion and community. Amen.

OPENING UP

Ask a participant to read the text on biblical prostitution. Then discuss and/or reflect on the following questions:

1. What negative impact does the Bible's association of female prostitutes with idolatry still have on women today?

2. Women have a lot of guilt and negative feelings about their bodies. In what ways is biblical tradition responsible for this? What can women do to overcome their feelings of guilt, low self-esteem, and shame?

Biblical Text Exploration

Read: Revelation 17:7-18

BACKGROUND

Biblical Prostitution

There were two kinds of prostitution in Israel. Secular or common prostitution involved only women. Sacred or cultic prostitution was performed by women and men. The former was immoral but legal. The latter was strictly prohibited on both moral and religious grounds, though it was practiced extensively in ancient Israel.

Prostitution was not illegal. But there was some social stigma attached to it, so male participants were usually discreet. Prostitutes were often social outcasts. They had to be unmarried because a married prostitute would be guilty of adultery, an offense that was punishable by death.

The two types of prostitution in Israel were described in two terms: *zona* for the female common harlot and *quades/qedesa* for the sacred or cult prostitution. Both were often interchanged in the narrative and prophetic writings, so that females, prostitutes, and idolatry became closely identified. The term "harlot" was used metaphorically by several prophets (i.e., Hosea) to describe Israel's recalcitrant relationship with God or a husband's relationship with an errant wife.

This extended a negative image to women well beyond simply prostitutes. So women, in general, particularly those of a different religion or culture, suffered gender discrimination in addition to the other types of discrimination that can affect them.[1]

QUESTIONS FOR DISCUSSION AND/OR INDIVIDUAL REFLECTION

1. Why is the whore more powerful than men and systems? What did she capitalize on to gain control over them?[2]

2. What happened to the whore at the end (v. 16)? Was this an im age symbolic of the fate of prostituted women in our times? Why?

3. In verse 17, John used God as the "initiator" of burning and cannibalizing the whore. How do you account for this?

Contextualization

Divide the participants into three groups. Each group will discuss a particular case of prostitution. Share your personal reactions. (Individual readers: Reflect on a selected case.)

Group 1

A fourteen-year-old girl prostitutes herself to support her boyfriend's heroin addiction. Later, she works the streets to support her own habit. She begins, like most teenage streetwalkers, to rely on a pimp for protection. She is uneducated and is frequently subjected to violence in her relationships and with her customers. Her job does not allow her to receive unemployment insurance, sick leave, or maternity leave, and most of all, she has no control over whether she has sex with a man. This is decided by a pimp.[3]

Group 2

Imagine the life of a Park Avenue call girl. Many call girls drift into prostitution not because of material want or lack of alternatives but because of their experience with multiple and promiscuous relationships. Some are young college graduates, who upon graduation earn money by prostitution while searching for other jobs. Call girls can earn thirty thousand to one hundred thousand dollars annually. These women have control over the entire amount they earn as well as a high degree of independence, far greater than that experienced in most other forms of work.[4]

Group 3

Prostitution in Asia is often associated with poverty. Take, for example, the Philippines, where almost five hundred thousand women work as prostitutes—either full time or part time to supplement other employment. They all run the risks of suffering from sexually transmitted diseases, psychological problems, and violence or death at the hands of their pimps, employers, or clients.[5]

Olongapo City must be a contender in any competition for the world's biggest brothel, with seventeen thousand prostitutes operating in this small city. The history of prostitution in Olongapo traces back to 1901 when U.S. President Roosevelt issued an executive order designating Subic Bay in Olongapo as a military reservation area. The city became a haven and a place of recreation for the sailors and other military personnel.[6]

Responding in Faith

How can we help these women become whole again?

A Moment of Reflection

SONG OF WHOLENESS

"Mantle of Light" (words and music: Colleen Fulmer, 1985) *or*

"Take My Life and Let It Be" (words: Frances Ridley Havergal, 1874; music: unknown) *or*

"I Love You, God, Who Heard My Cry" (words: Isaac Watts, 1719; music: African American spiritual; arr.: Richard Smallwood, 1975) *or*

"Healer of Our Every Ill" (words and music: Marty Haugen, 1987)

RESPONSIVE READING
An Outcast's Psalm

All: My God, my God, have pity on me for I am greatly afflicted.

Choir 1: My heart is heavy laden, my sorrow is like stone that weighs me down and paves the road on which I walk alone.

Choir 2: I live on the margins of meaning, an outcast forced to choose, above all else, survival. I have nothing to lose.

Choir 1: I hurry through public places, hard pressed to outrun my shame, fearing the pointed gossip that pierces me to blame.

Choir 2: Those who would call me sinner, fail to understand the burden of life I carry and never lend a hand.

Choir 1: My nights are filled with weeping, my days approach despair. How shall I sing the song I know is unwelcome everywhere?

Choir 2: I lift my life to your justice, I lift my love to your own, and wait on your word, like a lingering bird, when all of its flock have flown.

Choir 1: Let me touch the feet of your mercy, let me wash them with my tears. Let me hear your word of comfort dispelling all my fears.

Choir 2: Then my soul will sing of your goodness, and the earth will repeat the song, "til the sweet smelling oil of gladness anoints me and makes me strong."

Choir 1: My God, I am sorely afflicted. It is more than I can bear.

Choir 2: Deliver me from evil. Have pity and hear my prayer.

All: My God, my God, have pity on me, for I am greatly afflicted.[7]

CLOSING PRAYER
(in unison)

We (I) turn to you and your mercy, O God of barren places and friend of the oppressed. We (I) stand in need of conversion, from pain to peace, from sadness to joy, from guilt to affirmation. Lead us (me) not into isolation, but deliver us (me) from anger, for yours is the kindness, the patience, the strength we desire, now and forever, Amen.[8]

SENDING FORTH

"Thuma Mina" ("Send Me, Lord") words and music: Trad. South African *or*

"Go Now in Peace" (words and music: Natalie Sleeth, 1976)

Session Assessment

Evaluate your learnings and/or discernments.

Session 7

Seeking Refuge in the City

Revelation 18:1-20

After this I saw another angel coming down from heaven, having great authority; and the earth was made bright with his splendor. He called out with a mighty voice,

> "Fallen, fallen is Babylon the great!
>> It has become a dwelling place of demons,
> a haunt of every foul and hateful bird,
>> a haunt of every foul and hateful beast.
> For all the nations have drunk
>> of the wine of the wrath of her fornication,
> and the kings of the earth have committed fornication with her,
>> and the merchants of the earth have grown rich from the power of
>> her luxury."

Then I heard another voice from heaven saying,
> "Come out of her, my people,
>> so that you do not take part in her sins,
> and so that you do not share
>> in her plagues;
> for her sins are heaped high as heaven,
>> and God has remembered her iniquities.
> Render to her as she herself has rendered,
>> and repay her double for her deeds;

mix a double draught for her in the cup she mixed.
As she glorified herself and lived luxuriously,
    so give her a like measure of torment and grief.
Since in her heart she says,
    'I rule as a queen;
I am no widow,
    and I will never see grief,'
therefore her plagues will come in a single day—
    pestilence and mourning and famine—
and she will be burned with fire;
    for mighty is the Lord God who judges her."

And the kings of the earth, who committed fornication and lived in luxury with her, will weep and wail over her when they see the smoke of her burning; they will stand far off, in fear of her torment, and say,

"Alas, alas, the great city,
    Babylon, the mighty city!
For in one hour your judgment has come."

And the merchants of the earth weep and mourn for her, since no one buys their cargo anymore, cargo of gold, silver, jewels and pearls, fine linen, purple, silk and scarlet, all kinds of scented wood, all articles of ivory, all articles of costly wood, bronze, iron, and marble, cinnamon, spice, incense, myrrh, frankincense, wine, olive oil, choice flour and wheat, cattle and sheep, horses and chariots, slaves—and human lives.

"The fruit for which your soul longed
    has gone from you,
and all your dainties and your splendor
    are lost to you,
    never to be found again!"

The merchants of these wares, who gained wealth from her, will stand far off, in fear of her torment, weeping and mourning aloud,

"Alas, alas, the great city,
    clothed in fine linen,
        in purple and scarlet,
    adorned with gold,
        with jewels, and with pearls!
For in one hour all this wealth
    has been laid waste!"

And all shipmasters and seafarers, sailors and all whose trade is on the sea, stood far off and cried out as they saw the smoke of her burning, "What city was like the great city?"

And they threw dust on their heads, as they wept and mourned, crying out,

> *"Alas, alas, the great city,*
>> *where all who had ships at sea*
>> *grew rich by her wealth!*
> *For in one hour she has been laid waste.*
> *Rejoice over her, O heaven,*
>> *you saints and apostles and prophets!*
> *For God has given judgment for*
>> *you against her."*

Objectives

◆ To understand the meaning of the "city" as a female image in this particular text.

◆ To discover why refugees have come to the "city" to seek refuge and residence.

◆ To create an image of a city in which peace and justice reign.

Community Circle or Individual Centering

OPENING SONG

"Lead on O Cloud of Presence" (words: Ruth Duck, 1974; music: Henry Thomas Smart, 1836) *or*

"When I Needed a Neighbor" (words and music: Sidney Carter, 1962; harm.: in Cantate Domino) *or*

"In the Quiet Curve of Evening" (words and music: Julie Howard, 1993; arr.: Vera Lyons, 1993)

Opening Prayer

Well-traveled, wandering God of compassion,
as you have led your people to a land filled with milk and honey,
so we (I) invoke your guidance to the millions of refugees all over the
 world.
People in Rwanda, Bosnia, East Timor, Kosovo.
We (I) remember them in our (my) prayers that they may seek refuge
 in lands
where they would be welcomed.
In our gathering this day, fill us (me) with your Spirit
that we (I) may open our (my) heart(s) to the strangers in our (my)
 midst.
Fill us (me) with compassion to love the unloved neighbor.
make us (me) your instrument(s) for a community where love abounds.
Amen.

Opening Up: Listening to Vjosa's Story

Others on the List Were Not as Lucky . . .

Dr. Vjosa Dobruna traveled to Washington, D.C. to testify before the United States Senate on her experience of being forced from her home in Pristina.

My name is Dr. Vjosa Dobruna. As a pediatrician and human rights activist, I founded and direct the Center for Protection of Women and Children, a community clinic in Pristina, Kosovo. The Center works with war trauma victims, families in need and handicapped children. We also cooperate with international nongovernmental and private voluntary organizations to monitor humanitarian and human rights violations.

Pristina, which was a city of more than 200,000 inhabitants, now has a population of 15,000 to 20,000, mostly Serbs. I was among those forced to leave Pristina by Serbian security forces. Before forcing us out of town, Serbian security troops demanded money and beat us, both my sister and I. They beat my brother-in-law very badly, threatening his wife that they would kill him.

Even before I left Pristina, I had changed apartments every night for the previous six nights, ever since I was told by a friend that my name was on a list of targeted ethnic Albanians. Others on the list were not as lucky. Human rights lawyer Bajram Kelmendi, along with his two sons, was abducted by Serbian security or paramilitary forces in front of his wife and grandchildren. Serbian police told the family to kiss him good-bye, they would not see him again. Bajram's body was found three days later, on the road next to a gas station. He had been shot in the head repeatedly. His sons were killed with him.

After being ordered out of Pristina myself, I rode with my family to the border. I rode in the back of the car, covered by a sheet, so that police would not recognize me as a human rights activist. By the time we reached the long line of cars waiting to cross, we had seven adults and two children in the car. While in line, we were forced by Serbian police to keep the doors shut and windows closed for at least 24 hours; we waited in line for some 56 hours. As we waited, we saw many trains passing on the railway beside us, carrying thousands of refugees. We heard one man in the car behind us cry out, because he saw his elderly father in the crowded window of one passing train, headed for the Macedonian border. Hours later the trains would return empty.

When we finally reached the Blace border crossing at the border with Macedonia, the situation was inhuman. The flow of deportees into Blace seemed to be well-coordinated between the Serbian and Macedonian border guards. The deportees slept in the open, in an enormous muddy pit with little or no water or food for the first two days. There was no proper medical care, and international aid organizations were not permitted access to the camp by the Macedonian police.

I personally was kept from providing immediate aid to a seventeen-day-old infant suffering from severe dehydration.

The baby died.[1]

REFLECTION AND SHARING

A look at Vjosa's story draws us to the realization that refugees and immigrants in other parts of the world need our urgent attention to their plight for solidarity, love, and social justice. Cite ways in which we could offer our support to them.

Biblical Text Exploration

Read: Revelation 18:1-20

Background

Commentaries on Revelation: 18:1-20

Verses 1–3. The terrible price of sin: Babylon the city has become a source of evil spirits (anger, bitterness, disillusionment, the inability to forgive or let go of hurt) and for filthy residents (sinful habits, lust, alcoholism, overeating, etc.). Babylon becomes a cage that imprisons and will not let go of evil. "Alas, Babylon!" is an apt warning to humanity to choose good and not evil, lest eventually we should become possessed by evil.

Verses 4–8. The warning to God's people is to stay away from the cage in which Babylon is trapping herself. If we do not avoid the pitfalls, we will be trapped. Negative behavior carries its own punishment and if we want to avoid that punishment, we had better depart from the negative behavior and not let ourselves be fooled by the voices that promise bliss and deliver only misery.

Verses 9–10. There are four groups of mourners in the fall of Babylon. Those who mourn over the destruction of evil are of two kinds those who stood to benefit from the continuation of evil and those whose participation in it makes them fearful of a like fate. The first group of mourners are the kings, the power structures of the world. The breakdown of Rome's power leaves them unprotected with good reasons to fear retaliation from those they have oppressed. The result of power games in the world is often more divisive than unitive. The only union created is a union of force, a union of fear and one that will crumble once the power structure loses its backing. The kings have reason to mourn, since they imitated the ruthlessness of Rome, they can expect the same catastrophe for themselves as has befallen Rome.

Verses 11–14. The merchants join the dirge because they are losing their market, not because Babylon is afflicted. Here we have the mourning of "commercialism" and it is a self-centered mourning. When stability is destroyed, the merchants are likely to hurt in their pockets; hence, their reason for supporting any government that enables them to continue making money. Who can tell how many wars have been instigated in the world for the purpose of protecting the market of the merchants? The sad fact is that most wars have greed as one of their driving forces. There is a need to survive in the world, and each nation has the obligation to protect its economic structure, but this ought not to be done at the expense of other nations, especially of economically poorer nations.

Verses 15–17a. The next mourners are the modern equivalent of bankers and money-brokers of the world. The stock market is always in a precarious balance when the status quo begins to crumble. The speculators who live and get rich off the money of others are seen here as mourning the internal collapse of the power structure.

Verses 17b–19. The international traders now come forward to mourn. They are an integral part of the web and often the cause of so much human misery. From slave trading to setting up corporations in foreign countries and interfering with their internal politics, the international traders have often instigated wars and supported tyranny for the sake of the profit.

Verse 20. This verse is a message of vindication for God's people, the proof that it is God's way that works, not worldly greed. Just as four groups were called to mourn, four groups are called to rejoice. These might be divided into two groups of two: the heavens and the saints, the apostles and the prophets. The first refers to general categories; the second refers to the activities of the church. The heavens represent all the spiritual beings who carry out God's commandments and who oversee the activities of humanity, particularly the cosmic struggle. The saints are those who serve on the physical level of struggle. They are the holy people in the world, whether Christians or non-Christians, who are trying to accomplish God's will. The apostles are those who bear witness to Jesus, the preachers, the teachers, the inspirers of the church. The prophets are the workers on the level of economic and social justice. They are those who speak boldly for God's values and who challenge the injustices in the world. The destruction of Babylon will mean the reestablishment of that justice for which they spoke and for which the martyred died.[2]

QUESTIONS FOR DISCUSSION AND/OR INDIVIDUAL REFLECTION

1. Verses 1–3. These opening verses indicate that the great city Babylon has fallen. What possible reasons led Babylon to her downfall?

2. Verses 4–8. What was the warning all about in these particular verses?

3. Verses 9–19. The merchants, bankers, and international traders were mourning for Babylon's downfall. Why is this so?

4. Verse 20. What message of hope is cited in this text? To whom is it addressed?

5. What characteristics of a "city" nurture and give life to people? Can you see any of these characteristics in Babylon? Why or why not?

Contextualization

Divide the participants into three groups. Each group will be given a theme to discuss related to the issue of refugees and immigration.[3] (Individual readers: Select a reading for reflection.)

Group 1: "A Special Burden for Women"

During the second half of this century, the number of female migrants has increased all over the world. This phenomenon is connected with another, better known, but hardly resolved, that of poverty among women.

In exile, political or economic in origin, women are mostly ignored, ostracized, exploited, or else treated merely as people in need of assistance. Women are usually considered as just one component of the refugee or the immigrant problem. They are rarely viewed as partners in the search for a solution. They have been uprooted, their lives have been thrown into disorder and they probably suffer even more than men. Obliged by their traditional societies to maintain and reproduce its social patterns, yet confronted by the need to adapt to the host society, they are subject to particularly traumatic pressures. Consider the following:

1. It is estimated that ninety percent of Ethiopian refugees in Somalia are women and dependent children, and eighty percent of the Kampuchean shelters along the Thai borders are supervised by women, as are at least half of the Palestinian households in Lebanon.

2. The known effects of the dual burden assumed by gainfully employed women are amplified in the case of migrant workers. These effects are overwork, physical exhaustion, and mental problems. Let us also remember the women who are subjected to sexual abuse or forced, in order to survive, to become prostitutes. In most cases, these women are unaware of their rights or are not in a position to claim them.

Group 2: "The Cry of Embittered Youth"

Long after their parents leave their country, the young still crave to establish their identity. This is as true for the Syrians and Lebanese in Argentina, as it is for the Latin Americans in the United States, the Koreans in Japan, the Algerians in France, and the West Indians in Great Britain. To feel that they have to choose between the culture of their parents and that of the society in which they grow up is tearing apart many young second-generation migrants. It seems to them that in choosing one world they automatically exclude the other, whereas they themselves do not really belong to either. They feel that if they decide to become integrated and thus reject their culture of origin, they would most likely be cut off from their family, and if they were to be thrown out of the host country, they would have lost everything. If they were to abide by the norms and values of their society of origin, they would no longer be able to communicate with youth in the host country, and they would be completely isolated.

Violence often appears to be their way of expression because many young foreigners have not found any other means of expressing themselves. Tamils have been discriminated against in Sri Lanka and the younger generation has taken up arms. Maghrebans in France have been ostracized, and some young immigrants are attempting to offset the violence inflicted by a few by creating autonomous organizations to promote dialogue. West Indian communities in Great Britain have been housed in tumbledown areas where the unemployment rate for youth is extremely high and violent riots burst out periodically. Expression is not possible if no one is listening, if there is no partner. What the younger immigrants are claiming is no more than the right to be able to participate fully in the society they are living in, without giving up their own inherent characteristics.

Group 3: "Racism: The Snake in the Grass"

The presence of millions of foreigners in many countries raises problems of coexistence that are not easy to resolve because economic difficulties would make it seem as if nationals and foreigners are in competition with each other, and it gives rise to simplistic rationalizations. Aliens, be they refugees or immigrants, are now being labeled "unassimilable" or "culturally incompatible" because of the secret fear that their high birth rate might endanger the "purity" of the nation.

From ignorance to spitefulness, from chauvinism to racist assaults, the process of rejection of "foreign elements" is varied. It is important to discover where and how racism develops even in circumstances that appear to be acceptable to society. Ostracized and consequently cast aside, aliens are seen as potential threats to security. When the immigrants become settled, organized and established, and start procreating, when their presence is felt, xenophobia (fear or dislike of strangers or foreigners) sets in. Such sentiments are closely allied to the world economic imbalance, which has created such a huge gap between rich and poor countries and implanted in the rich the irrational but ever-present fear that masses of starving and unemployed people will suddenly arrive on their shores.

Racism establishes fundamental differences and a hierarchy among ethnic groups and, in this way, justifies not only rejection, but also domination and exploitation of one group by another. The danger is the greatest when the ideological and political theories of a society appear to provide a seemingly coherent framework for popular emotional reactions. It then becomes political racism that leads to violence and criminal acts and, consequently, segregation. Racism is not primarily a personal pathological condition but a perversion of economic and social origin.

QUESTION FOR DISCUSSION IN EACH GROUP

What issues are raised in each particular theme?

Responding in Faith

Reflect on the sociopolitical and cultural situations in your own city. Is this your vision of an ideal city in which foreigners, refugees, and immigrants can live securely?

A Moment of Reflection

SONG OF SOLIDARITY

"God, Mother of Exiles" (words and music: Colleen Fulmer, 1985; text of refrain by Emma Lazarus) *or*

"When a Poor One" (Spanish words and music: J. A. Olivar and Miguel Manzano, 1976; trans.: George Lockwood, 1989; arr.: Alvin Schutmaat) *or*

"Homeless People, Will You Listen?" (words: Walter Farquharson, 1977; music: Ron Klusmeier, 1977)

RECITE
I Am No Longer Afraid of Death

I am no longer afraid of death; I know well its dark
and cold corridors leading to life . . .
I am afraid rather of that life
which does not come out of death
which cramps our hands and retards our march . . .
I am afraid of my fear, and even more of the fear of others,
who do not know where they are going,
who continue clinging to what they consider to be life
which we know to be death!
I live each day to kill death;
I live each day to beget life, and in this dying unto death,
I die a thousand times and am reborn another thousand
through that love from my People, which nourishes hope![4]

MEDITATION
(all in silence)

Voice: I am a refugee. There are fifteen million of us in the world. Eighty percent of us are women and children. I am your kinswoman fleeing Afghanistan, Ethiopia, Vietnam, Guatemala, El Salvador. I have little voice in the refugee camps . . . in the governments. We had to flee our homes at night and I have nothing but my clothes. Will you share my story?[5]

A minute of silent prayer for all refugees in the world.

CLOSING PRAYER
(in unison)

O God, may you grant us (me) hope in the flame of wisdom we (I) have lit on this solemn night, trusting in one another and building solidarity with all who form the webwork of peace and justice, that we (I) may open our doors to strangers and refugees. Amen.

Session Assessment

Evaluate your learnings and/or discernments.

Session 8

The Bride

Revelation 19:7-8; 21:2-4, 9-10; 22:17

Let us rejoice and exult
*   and give him the glory,*
for the marriage of the Lamb has come,
*   and his bride has made herself ready;*
to her it has been granted to be clothed
*   with fine linen, bright and pure"—*
for the fine linen is the righteous deeds of the saints.

And I saw the holy city, the new Jerusalem, coming down out of heaven
from God, prepared as a bride adorned for her husband. And I heard a
loud voice from the throne saying,

"See, the home of God is among mortals.
He will dwell with them as their God;
they will be his peoples,
and God himself will be with them;
he will wipe every tear from their eyes.
Death will be no more;
mourning and crying and pain will be no more,
for the first things have passed away."

Then one of the seven angels who had the seven bowls full of the seven
last plagues came and said to me, "Come, I will show you the bride, the wife

of the Lamb." And in the spirit he carried me away to a great, high mountain and showed me the holy city Jerusalem coming down out of heaven from God.

> *The Spirit and the bride say, "Come."*
> *And let everyone who hears say, "Come."*
> *And let everyone who is thirsty come.*
> *Let anyone who wishes take the water of life as a gift.*

Objectives

❧ To understand the metaphoric and realistic meanings of the word "bride" as presented in the texts.

❧ To look into the meaning of "marriage" as a God-people covenant.

❧ To discuss some marital issues that affect women today.

Community Circle or Individual Centering

OPENING SONG OF LOVE

"Blessed Is She" (words and music: Colleen Fulmer, 1985) *or*

"In Loving Partnership" (words and music: Jim Strathdee, 1982) *or*

"Love Divine, All Love's Excelling" (words: Charles Wesley, 1747; music: Rowland Huw Prichard, 1831)

OPENING PRAYER

O God, our (my) lover.
We (I) cling ourselves (myself) to you as a bride marries a groom.
You have called us (me) into covenant with you, no matter who and what we are (I am).
We (I) acknowledge your unconditional love that is freely given to us (me) through Jesus the Christ. In this love, we (I) are (am) able to extend our (my) hands to others.
May we (I) continue to nourish this spirit of togetherness that brings us (me) into constant relationship with you. Amen.

Opening Up: "Bible Drill"

Divide the participants into two groups. Each member in each group should have a Bible. The facilitator will ask each participant to locate some verses in the Bible that reflect woman-man relationships. The first one to locate the verse wins a point for her group. The text will be read once more. Think of a word that describes the covenant between God and human beings as expressed in the verses. (Individual readers: Select a scripture passage.)

Suggested Verses (Note: The facilitator has the option to select verses for this activity.)

Genesis 2:23–24	(Eve and Adam)
Genesis 17:15	(Sarah and Abraham)
Ruth 4:13	(Ruth and Boaz)
Song of Solomon 4:9–10	(Bride and Bridegroom)
Hosea 3:1–3	(Gomer and Hosea)
Luke 2:4–7	(Mary and Joseph)
Luke 7:44–47	(The Sinful Woman and Jesus)
Luke 8:47–48	(The Sick Woman and Jesus)
Luke 18:1–8	(The Persistent Widow and the Judge)
John 4:7–10	(The Samaritan Woman and Jesus)

Biblical Text Exploration

Read: Revelation 19:7-8; 21:2-4; 9-10; 22:17

Background: What Do Women Theologians Say about These Texts?

Reading 1

The announcement of Babylon's fall and of the vindication of the saints causes rejoicing in heaven (19:5). This heavenly song quickly moves into one of celebration for the imminent marriage of the Lamb and the "bride" (19:6–8) . . . (as an antithesis to the whore), the bride of the Lamb is clothed with "fine linen, bright and pure" (19:8). After this brief anticipation of the appearance of the "bride" follow successive visions of the warrior Messiah, the capture of the beasts, the resurrection, the millennial reign of those martyred for Jesus, the release and the defeat of Satan, the second resurrection, and the judgment (19:9—20:15).

Then at last, the New Jerusalem appears, "coming down out of heaven from God, prepared as a bride adorned for her husband" (21:2). Here John has blended the conventional motif of a new Jerusalem, kept in heaven until the last days, with the metaphor of the church—the people of God—as the bride of Christ. Indeed, the New Jerusalem envisioned by John is itself a metaphor for the people of God: the bride's "fine linen, bright and pure" is said to be "the righteous deeds of the saints" (19:8).

The bride metaphor . . . functioned especially well in the patriarchal culture of the first century, which placed a high premium on the strict management of women's sexuality. In this culture the ideal bride was a "pure" virgin who had no interests or liaisons that would compromise her loyalty to her husband (2 Cor. 11:2).[1]

Reading 2

The "new heaven and earth" stand in continuity with the former heaven and earth, but they form a qualitatively new and unified world. This new reality is characterized by God's presence among the peoples of God. The vision of the New Jerusalem, arrayed like a bride in the splendor of the "righteous deeds of the saints," makes symbolically present God's eschatological salvation and reign which require that heaven will move down to earth. . . .

Revelation's vision of salvation centers on the earth. Christ's and God's rule and power cannot coexist with the dehumanizing power that corrupt and devastate the earth (19:2). The outcries of the persecuted for the enactment of justice and judgment therefore also rise up on behalf of the earth as God's creation. God's justice and judgment bring not only vindication of those persecuted and murdered, but also engenders total human well-being and salvation on earth. Not suffering, weeping, mourning, hunger, captivity and death, but rather life, light, and happiness determine the reality of the new heaven and earth. . . . The future intended world of God's salvation is not envisioned as an island but as encompassing all of creation.[2]

Reading 3

In all of these metaphors of the religious body as female, the Goddess is captured and subdued and molded . . . to fit male fantasies of the ideal female. The Bride is adorned, in contrast to the stripping and burning of the Whore. The marriage of the Bride counters the death of the Whore. The ancient Goddess in all her characteristic diversity of motherhood, erotic sexuality, virginity, and as a warrior, justice giver, caretaker, creatrix of nature and arts, and destroyer is segmented into these binary oppositions of good and evil, whore and virgin-mother. The goddess (woman?) is compartmentalized and stereotyped. . . . I find in Revelation only negative and male-dominated images of women. The maternal and bridal images are so often the points of redeeming this text for women, but both these images are patriarchal and heterosexists. In general, readings of Revelation ignore the gender roles and focus on the political implications. A political reading using liberation theology does reveal the call to endurance and hope in Revelation, and this reading is important.[3]

Reading 4

The new heaven and the new earth—the new consciousness of Life—is represented as a reuniting of male and female from Genesis 1:27. Ruach Elohiym (the Spirit/breath of God) has moved upon the waters of all consciousness, all history, all life, all men and women, in male and female symbols of utmost purity. . . . [This is] the holy city prepared as a bride adorned for her husband.[4]

QUESTIONS FOR DISCUSSION AND/OR INDIVIDUAL REFLECTION

1. Who is the Bride? the Lamb? What does the marriage symbolize (Rev. 19:7–8)?

2. What is the New Jerusalem? What kind of a dwelling place is this? What message of hope is shown in these verses (Rev. 21:2–4, 9–10)?

3. What characteristics of the "bride" are depicted in these texts? Are these suggestive of our society's expectations of women? How are these images being affirmed or distorted?

Contextualization

Read the following anecdote shared by Judy Marchand, an activist and a potter from Brandon, Manitoba, on the life of her mother:

My mother was a strong woman. She had twelve children. When we lived in towns where there was no running water or electricity, she heated water from the pump and washed clothes by hand. Usually there was a baby. When she was trying to remember the date of an event, she would say, "Now who was the baby then?" One year, four of us had measles at the same time. We stayed in bed in a darkened room. Every now and then, Mom would come in with water, soup, and cool hands.

Her hands were always busy. In the fall, the house was filled with smells of spices and simmering fruit as she made up a winter's supply of pickles, relish and jams. In September, she would begin knitting our toques, mittens and scarves for the winter.

Sometimes she would lose her patience and yell at us, but it would blow over. I don't remember her spanking us. She read the newspaper closely and listened to the radio. She could get really worked up about political events.

When I became active in the women's movement, there were many issues on which my mother and I did not agree. Yet my sense of what was possible had been formed by seeing her do what she had to do. My mother's commitment had been to keep her family going in the face of poverty and isolation: my commitment was to be part of changing the way women could live their lives.

Recently, my mother's busy hands and active mind have been quieted by several small strokes. At eighty-three, she has become childlike. I go to her hospital room and brush her hair, help her to walk, get her ready for bed and reassure her that she is loved and will be cared for. At times, I feel I am my mother's mother.[5]

QUESTIONS FOR DISCUSSION AND/OR INDIVIDUAL REFLECTION

1. In the story read, name some important issues that may affect women in their marriage. What issues do you think are in need of our urgent attention?

2. How is Judy Marchand's loving and caring mother compared to God's relationship with us?

Responding in Faith

Cite ways the issues mentioned can empower mothers or wives in enhancing a "life-giving" marriage.

A Moment of Reflection

SONG OF COVENANT

"This Ancient Love" (words and music: Carolyn McDade, 1988) *or*

"O Perfect Love" (words: Dorothy Frances Gurney, 1883; music: Joseph Barnby, 1889) *or*

"O Love That Wilt Not Let Me Go" (words: George Matheson, 1881; music: Albert Lister Peace, 1884)

Responsive Reading: A Psalm of Love

Choir 1: I love you, O God, with all my heart and with the whole of my being.

Choir 2: Wide open am I to love and be loved, because you have first loved me.

Choir 1: Daily I seek to share that love, as I touched the lives of others.

Choir 2: Daily I see and receive that love, as others reached out to me.

Choir 1: Teach me to serve you generously, as a sign of love extended.

Choir 2: Teach me to sit at the feet of your word made love in history.

Choir 1: Your love is a friend who is there for me, in the silence of my mourning.

Choir 2: Your love is a resurrected hope, to one well beyond surprise.

All: Love grows greater by loving you, and loving one another. Love grows bigger and better by living the love that never dies.[6]

One-Sentence Prayers for All Married Women
(by the participants)

Session Assessment

Evaluate your learnings and/or discernments.

Session 9

God as Midwife of Creation

Revelation 21:1-5, 22-27

Then I saw a new heaven and a new earth; for the first heaven and the first earth had passed away, and the sea was no more. And I saw the holy city, the new Jerusalem, coming down out of heaven from God, prepared as a bride adorned for her husband. And I heard a loud voice from the throne saying,

> *"See, the home of God is among mortals.*
> *He will dwell with them as their God;*
> *they will be his peoples,*
> *and God himself will be with them;*
> *he will wipe every tear from their eyes.*
> *Death will be no more;*
> *mourning and crying and pain will be no more,*
> *for the first things have passed away."*

I saw no temple in the city, for its temple is the Lord God the Almighty and the Lamb. And the city has no need of sun or moon to shine on it, for the glory of God is its light, and its lamp is the Lamb. The nations will walk by its light, and the kings of the earth will bring their glory into it. its gates will never be shut by day—and there will be no night there. People will bring into it the glory and the honor of the nations. But nothing unclean will enter it, nor anyone who practices abomination or falsehood, but only those who are written in the Lamb's book of life.

Objectives

> To help the participants understand the symbolic meaning of 'ecofeminism' interpreted in the text as God's midwifing the whole of creation in pursuit of the New Jerusalem.

> To describe the transformation of the earth inhabited by the "newness" of creation.

> To make a covenant in saving Mother Earth.

Community Circle or Individual Centering

OPENING SONG

"Alter Christus" (words and music: Colleen Fulmer, 1985) *or*

"Morning Has Broken" (words: Eleanor Farjeon, 1931; music: Gaelic melody) *or*
"For the Beauty of the Earth" (words: Folliott Sandford Pierpoint, 1864; music: David Evans, 1927)

OPENING PRAYER

Creative, creating God,
you have made us (me) in your image,
you have blessed us (me) in union with the mother earth.
You bring forth life from land, skies, and seas.
you have taught us (me) to respect all creation,
knowing that these sacred gifts are from your loving, creative hands.
Make us (me) in partnership with the earth
and share in the labor of giving birth to new life.
We (I) praise your name in all creations. Amen.

OPENING UP

Reflect on one of the following questions by writing your thoughts or share your musings with the group.

1. How do you experience an interconnection with the joys and the power of God as creator?

2. How is God depicted as midwife of creation?

3. Do you see yourself as a cocreator with God? What images bring you to this realization?

4. How can you restore the earth's dignity?

Biblical Text Exploration

Read: Revelation 21:1-5, 22-27

BACKGROUND

The Liberated World of God

The "first" heaven and earth now belongs to the past, since they were determined by the antagonistic dualism between the reign of God and Christ in heaven and that of the dragon and his allies on earth and in the underworld. The "new heaven and earth" stand in continuity with the former heaven and earth, but they form a qualitatively new and unified world. This new reality is characterized by God's presence among the peoples of God. The vision of the New Jerusalem, arrayed like a bride in the splendor of the "righteous deeds of the saints," makes symbolically present God's eschatological salvation and reign which require that heaven will move down to earth.

Revelation's vision of salvation centers on the earth. God's rule cannot coexist with the dehumanizing power that corrupt and devastate the earth. The outcries of the persecuted for the enactment of justice and judgment also rise up on behalf of the earth as God's creation. God's justice and judgment bring not only vindication of those persecuted and murdered but also engenders total human well-being and salvation on earth. Not suffering, weeping, mourning, hunger, captivity and death, but rather life, light and happiness determine reality of the new heaven and earth. Therefore the place of beasts and symbol of evil no longer exists. The future intended world of God's salvation is not envisioned as an island but as encompassing all of creation.

It is God who makes everything new. Those who will remain victorious will be the heirs of God's liberated world. Those who participate in the destructive praxis of the anti-divine, oppressive powers will suffer the second death of eternal punishment.[1]

QUESTIONS FOR DISCUSSION AND/OR INDIVIDUAL REFLECTION

1. In your point of view, what was the first heaven and earth like? How would this be different from the new heaven and the new earth as described in this text?

2. How will God relate to the people in this new creation?

3. Who will be the citizens of this new society? Why do you think so?

4. Why is there no "temple" in this new society? What does it mean for God to be the "temple"?

5. How is God characterized as midwife of the new creation? In the book of Isaiah, there are images of God as a midwife (66:9); a nursing mother (49:14–15); a woman in labor and again a nursing mother (66:7–13). Read these passages and reflect on them. What do they say about God?

Contextualization

Read this selection from "Cherishing the Earth" written by Martha Ann Kirk and Coral Nunnery. (Individual readers: Read silently or recite.)

First Reader:

In the beginning God created the heavens and the earth.
The earth was without form and void, and darkness was on the face of the deep; and the Spirit of God was moving over the face of the waters.
And God said, "Let there be light;" and there was light.
And God saw that the light was good! God divided light from darkness and called light, "day" and darkness, "night."
Evening came and morning came: the first day.
In the following days, God divided the heaven and earth, and called forth the dry land. And God saw that it was good.
And God created vegetation; seed-bearing plants, and fruit trees—so many varieties and shapes and colors.
And God saw that it was good.
Then God created the sun, the moon and the stars.
And God created the living creatures; birds to fly, and great sea serpents and all creatures that live in the water.
And God created the living creatures that live on the land.
God saw that it was good.
And God created man and woman, and blessed them, giving to them the gifts of the earth.
And the whole of creation was in balance.
And each part of creation had a contribution to make.
Each part of creation depended on the rest for what it needed.
And indeed, it was good. It was very good.
For generations and generations, we have lived with the land.
And it was good, it was very good.
There was harmony among all earth's creatures. The land provided all we needed—food, clothing, and shelter. We cared for the land, tenderly. The gifts of the land, the wonders and miracles of creation pointed us toward the Creator. We were part of the earth, one with the earth; not separate from or dominating over it.
We rejoiced in the earth and the gifts of the earth.
We had glad hearts and made merry.
All the tribes from the East and the West, the North and the South celebrated the goodness of creation. The earth had given forth wine and fruits in abundance.

We celebrated with our timbrels and lyres and had great festivals.
We had glad hearts. We had glad hearts. We had glad hearts.

Second Reader:

But through the ages, we have not cared for the earth as we should.
The prophets have long cried out at our abuse; we hear this in the words
of Isaiah. Read Isaiah 24:4–8 "the earth is polluted by its inhabitants."
For the earth is ravaged.
The earth is dying—dying.
We have poisoned our waters and air.
Destruction of forests and other habitats is driving one hundred species
of plants and animals to extinction every day. The losses are especially
serious in the tropical forests.
These forests cover only seven percent of the earth's surface, but
between fifty and eighty percent of the planet's species live there. The
genetic material being lost forever may contain secrets for fighting
diseases or improving crops.
Emissions of carbon dioxide and other greenhouse gases are raising the
atmosphere's mean temperature. If these emissions are not curtailed,
the temperature could rise as much as eighty degrees Farenheit in the
next sixty years. Main sources of carbon dioxide are the cars, factories,
and power plants of the industrial countries.
Another major source is the burning of tropical forests in the less developed world. Carbon emissions from Brazil alone are estimated at three
hundred thirty-six million tons per year.
Nations produce millions of tons of household garbage and toxic
industrial waste.
The world is running out of places to dispose of the refuse. The danger
to human health is rising rapidly. The throwaway societies of the developed countries generate the most trash. In New York, it is estimated that
one person's garbage is four pounds per day. Developing nations have
problems because they lack technology to dispose of hazardous chemi-
cal waste safely.
The people of the earth no longer live in harmony with the planet. The
waters are poisoned. The fish are dying. We cannot live without clean
water. And we grieve.
The air is poisoned—polluted. The ozone layer is depleted. We cannot
live without clean air. And we grieve.
Garbage litters our beaches; we have no place to dispose of raw sewage
and other wastes. Countless species of plants and animals are becoming
extinct. They can no longer live without clean air and water.

We have injured the earth's environment.
We are grieving.
We are grieving the loss of that which is most precious to us.
And we grieve.[2]

Responding in Faith

From the reading, share a symbol depicting your relationship with Mother Earth. (Individual readers: Share your symbol by writing about it in your journal.)

A Moment of Reflection

SONG ABOUT MOTHER EARTH

"God Who Gardens" (words and music: Colleen Fulmer, 1989) *or*

"To Show by Touch and Word" (words: Fred Kaan; music: Ron Klusmeier, 1974) *or*

"Touch the Earth Lightly" (words: Shirley Erena Murray, 1991; music: Collin Gibson, 1991) *or*

"The Earth and All Who Breathe" (words: Ruth Duck, 1983; music: attrib. J. S. Bach, 1736)

RESPONSIVE READING

A Psalm Proclaiming a Vision

Voice: Women, tell me, what do you see? Will there be a New Creation?

All: We see a new day dawning, with clean water, virgin forests, and fields of grain; trees are doing a ring dance in praise of God, in praise of Gaia; we are like children and all of us are walking in the rain.

Voice: Women, tell me, what do you see? Describe the New Creation.

All: We see a new age dawning, when no one will be hungry, when all will be sheltered and safe and secure and all of our work will be done, and all who praise Sophia will be sitting in the sun.

Voice: Women, tell me, what do you see? Are we the New Creation?

All: We see a new beginning in all who overcome addiction, in all who will not go to war, in all those good and generous ones who witness to compassion, who struggle to bring about a time when no one is below another and no one is above, when we are all within Shalom, bonded together in love.[3]

CLOSING PRAYER
(in unison)

Blessed are you, Source of Nourishment, for creating these fruits of the earth and sharing manna with your people as they wandered in the desert. Air, fire, water, earth, and spirit combined to make this food. Numberless beings have died and labored that we may eat. Nourish us (me) with the power of creation that we (I) may nourish life. Amen.[4]

Session Assessment

Evaluate your learnings and/or discernments.

Session 10

Women and Utopia[1]

Revelation 22:1-5

Then the angel showed me the river of the water of life, bright as crystal, flowing from the throne of God and of the Lamb through the middle of the street of the city. On either side of the river, is the tree of life with its twelve kinds of fruit, producing its fruit each month; and the leaves of the tree are for the healing of the nations. Nothing accursed will be found there any more. But the throne of God and of the Lamb will be in it, and his servants will worship him; they will see his face, and his name will be on their foreheads.

Objectives

❧ To understand the meaning of an alternative society (utopia) for women based on the text.

❧ To affirm women's participation in envisioning and achieving this new order of society.

Community Circle or Individual Centering

A Song of Empowerment for Women

"Mountain Moving Women" (words and music: Sandi Moore, 1989) *or*

"I See a New Heaven" (words and music: Carolyn McDade, 1979; harm.: Janet McGaughey, 1991) *or*

"Spirit Dancing" (words: Walter Farquharson, 1989; music: Lori Erhardt, 1988; arr.: Kenneth Gray, 1980) *or*

"Choose Life" (words and music: Colleen Fulmer, 1985)

OPENING PRAYER

O God of empowered and voiceless women,
you shake us (me) from our (my) slumber
and bring us (me) face to face with our (my) visions and dreams.
Make us (me) strong and courageous to resist evil in all forms
that we (I) may attain a "utopian" society where everyone is freed
from oppressive powers.
Mend our (my) broken communities with your healing power.
And liberate us (me) from the prison of male-domination.
Through Jesus, the champion of women's rights. Amen.

OPENING UP

Share an experience with the group of how you were put down because you are a woman. What do you think are the factors that brought you to that particular situation? How do you feel about it?

BIBLICAL TEXT EXPLORATION

Read: Revelation 22:1-5
Background

The utopian vision is not some idealistic trance that requires distance from political reality. Rather, the utopian vision is the motor of the notion of desire and freedom, and the final wish-fulfillment of the oppressed. The reality of hunger, political oppression, and economic deprivation drives humanity to the brink of History, and there is found the desire for the transformation of the world.[2]

QUESTIONS FOR DISCUSSION AND/OR INDIVIDUAL REFLECTION

1. What kind of community is pictured in verses 1–2? Where will this be lived out? Why do you think so?

2. Who will be the residents of this new community?

3. What do you think it would be like to live without pain, fear, or death, and with the continual direct presence of God? Will we ever come to realize this "whole new world"? How?

Contextualization

Discuss (or write in your journal) how the increasing cutbacks from the government affect women in general. With these oppressive socioeconomic and political conditions, it is difficult for us to achieve utopia. Is there a way we can create an alternative society for women? How?

Responding in Faith

Read the following essay, "Women and Utopia." Meditate on it and, in silence, remember those women who are suffering from the oppressive systems that brought them to destituteness and poverty.

Women and Utopia
(A response to Tina Pippin's challenge in *Death and Desire*)

Over the centuries, the situation of women is a living reality of male-dominated images. Every day we learn about women in their suffering and agony because of war and militarization; of women turning into prostitutes and domestic slaves because of economic poverty and inequality of pay and job opportunities; of women in abusive situations, raped and assaulted in their homes, workplaces, and in some public and private domains.

Moreover, women are victims in a culture of "machismo." Media advertising is full of images of the "real men" surrounded by an entourage of meagerly clad women of beauty. Movies idolize the "long-suffering" heroine patiently waiting for her male-deliverer, while the aggressive female is portrayed as a villain who destroys the life of the hero through seduction and deception. The church is also responsible for treating women as second-class citizens. Some Christian churches do not allow women to be ordained as priests or ministers because of fundamental biblical teachings and doctrines. They deprive women of preaching in the pulpit or administering in the sacraments. The only place allowed for women is the Sunday school, or the kitchen, or the nursery.

Truly, these images are painful and depressing. But amidst these squalid pictures are moments of resistance and hope. The spirit of women-rising is essential in the Book of Revelation. In Tina Pippin's *Death and Desire*, the Apocalypse as resistance literature has an important message in certain oppressive political and cultural contexts. It embraces the desire for Utopia—for a new heaven and a new earth. It is about God's time in which justice for the oppressed and judgment against the oppressors will not wait. The desire for a Utopian society is the dream of every woman who struggles in search for the wholeness of life. With every woman-rising and empowerment, the new heaven and new earth may sooner emerge; with women anointed by their own liberation process narrating the Good News; telling their own stories of freedom to everyone; how their broken lives were healed by building a new community; their freedom from captivity and second-rate citizenship; their process of "letting-go" of themselves from the prison of male-domination toward becoming equal partners in transforming the society.

Aspiring for Utopia is a difficult and a continuing task for women. Pippin explicitly asserts that: "To imagine the confrontation of good and evil (oppressed and oppressor), and the defeat of the enemy is a powerful experience. Foundations are shaken, cultural norms are questioned, the dominant ideology is ruptured. It is about the revolutionary event of the creation of God's Utopia."[3]

The Apocalypse writer (John) brings us to an alternative society that can be achieved through violence, murder, torture, hunger, pestilence, and destruction. It is a war of bloodshed and death. I disagree with his stand. I believe that women do not rejoice in this kind of struggle. Women do not desire martyrdom, violence, and dehumanization because it allows patriarchal abuse as exemplified by the stories of the four feminine images in the book of Revelation. Women must be involved in peaceful but vigilant undertakings in creating a utopian society.

Recognizing this alternative step, the need for a support system must be first in the list. We must support government and nongovernment organizations committed to initiating programs for women's liberation. We must persist in the proliferation of feminist advocacy and the increase of nationwide and global awareness of women's rights and issues. It is also imperative that we declare our strong solidarity with all women in their painful struggle for a fuller humanity, denouncing all forms of evil that subjugate them. Tina Pippin poses a challenge to every woman when she said, "Women in the Apocalypse are silenced, but women readers today have voices to speak to, of, and about the biblical and contemporary apocalypses. We need to develop voices of APOCALYPTIC THUNDER!"[4]

In response, we echo the message of a Filipina poet when she said:

> From womb to womb, we labour on giving.
> From chore to chore, we define loving.
> Our past is one long thread sewing our
> present and hemming our future.
> Who are we? What are our dreams?
> WE ARE LEADING WOMEN—WOMEN WHO HAVE FOUND OUR
> TRUE SELVES IN THE DRAMA OF MAKING HISTORY!
> To war, we respond with life.
> To atrocity, we unleash justice.
> To inequity, we thunder with liberation.
> We are leading the way to prepare
> the soil for our peoples feast.[5]

A Moment of Reflection

RECITE
(*privately and corporately*)

We (I) have a dream that one day soon . . .
we (I) women/woman will be honored, respected and loved, because you and I are equals created in the image of God;
There will no longer be a sexual double standard;
There will be equal sharing of domestic responsibilities;
There will be equal pay for work of equal status among women and men; We (I), who have been relegated to the home, will no longer be confined. There will be more women pastors, priests, moderators, and bishops. We (I), who make up the bulk of the silent majority, will no longer be silent. In unity, we (I) will raise our (my) voice(s), gather our (my) strength and offer our (my) lives (life) for world peace.[6]

SONG OF EMPOWERMENT FOR WOMEN

"Walls That Divide" (words: Walter Farquharson; music: Ron Klusmeier, 1974) *or*

"Now There Is No Male or Female" (words: Lynette Miller, 1986; music: 17th century German Catholic melody) *or*

"God Is Passionate Life" (words and music: Colleen Fulmer, 1985)

Reflection

Reader 1:

"Truly I say to you, those who say to this mountain, 'Be taken up and cast into the sea,' and do not doubt in their hearts, but believe that what they say will come to pass, it will be done for them. Therefore, I tell you, whatever you ask in prayer, believe that you receive it and you will" (Mark 11:23–24; Matt. 21:21; 17:20).

Reader 2:

As we stand before the mountains of educational, social, and psychological obstacles keeping women trapped in low-paying jobs, do we have faith? As we stand before the mountainous stockpiles of our nuclear arsenals, do we have faith? As we stand before the mountains of prejudice that keep women of the world from having any more than fifteen percent of the seats in national legislatures, do we have faith?

(*moment of silence*)

Reader 1:

After Jesus speaks of moving mountains, he continues: "And whenever you stand praying, forgive, if you have anything against anyone; so that your Father (God) in heaven may also forgive you your trespasses" (Mark 11:25).

Reader 2:

Do we have the forgiving love not to carry the grudges against our oppressors that keep us from moving on freely? Do we have the forgiving love to condemn the sinful systems, but not reject the sinners? Do we have the forgiving love not to let petty things divide us from each other in the struggle for justice?

(*moment of silence*)[7]

CLOSING PRAYER
(recite aloud)

Rise up, O God of Death-to-Life, and carry us all with you; from the tomb of our affliction into your brand new day, where there is no more keeping down or holding back, passing over any person, no more discrimination, but in the fullness of Your justice, all are equal, women and men, and all are one in you. Amen.[8]

Session Assessment

Evaluate your learnings and/or discernments.

Session II

Women Worship

A Closing Liturgy

Lighting of the Candle

Moments of Reflection

Leader: We are always starting over.
We are always beginning again.
Something within us changes.
It is time to be moving on . . .
May God grace all our turning points
with patience and peace.[1]

Opening Song

"Daughters of Miriam" (words and music: Colleen Fulmer, 1986) *or*

"Open My Eyes That I May See" (words and music: Clara Scott, 1895) *or*

"I'm Gonna Live So God Can Use Me" (words and music: African American spiritual; arr.: Wendel Whalum) *or*

"Come and Find the Quiet Center" (words: Shirley Erena Murray, 1989; music: attrib. Benjamin Franklin White, 1844; harm.: Ronald A. Nelson, 1978)

OPENING PRAYER
(*to be led by one person*)

Responsive Reading: A Psalm for Women Church

Leader: Grace and peace be to you, sisters of Elizabeth and Mary.

People: Blessing and power of spirit-church, be with all women of God.

Leader: How good and wholesome and holy it is for women to come together!

People: We share our sacred stories; sift through our grace experiences, and discover common ground.

Leader: Create our creeds of courage and our paradigms of praise.

People: We hear one another into being, laugh into life our sterile dreams, support the choice taking shape within us.

Leader: Women together share new life and celebrate miracles!

People: Share how the barren bring to birth, share the first fruits of believing.

Leader: Share all the many and marvelous ways the Spirit impregnates the women with the seeds of the new creation and the potential for significant change.

People: Old and young, ordinary women together break the grounds for a new world order that include the fringe of society, is rooted and grounded in justice, and grows strong in the embrace of peace.

All: Our soul sings in the strength of Shaddai, our spirit rejoices in Her creation. Amen.[2]

SPECIAL SONG
(*sing or recite the lyrics to one
of the above songs or another familiar song*)

Scripture Readings

Reading 1: Revelation 2:20–24—"The Woman Prophet Jezebel"

"But I have this against you: you tolerate that woman jezebel, who calls herself a prophet and is teaching and beguiling my servants to practice fornication and to eat food sacrificed to idols. I gave her time to repent, but she refuses to repent of her fornication. Beware, I am throwing her on a bed,

and those who commit adultery with her I am throwing into great distress, unless they repent of her doings; and I will strike her children dead. And all the churches will know that I am the one who searches minds and hearts, and I will give to each of you as your works deserve. But to the rest of you in Thyatira, who do not hold this teaching, who have not learned what some call 'the deep things of Satan,' to you I say, I do not lay on you any other burden. . . . "

Reading 2: Revelation 12:1–8—"The Woman Clothed With the Sun"

A great portent appeared in heaven: a woman clothed with the sun, with the moon under her feet, and on her head a crown of twelve stars. She was pregnant and was crying out in birthpangs, in the agony of giving birth. Then another portent appeared in heaven: a great red dragon, with seven heads and ten horns, and seven diadems on his heads. His tail swept down a third of the stars of heaven and threw them to the earth. Then the dragon stood before the woman who was about to bear a child, so that he might devour her child as soon as it was born. And she gave birth to a son, a male child, who is to rule all the nations with a rod of iron. But her child was snatched away and taken to God and to his throne; and the woman fled into the wilderness, where she has a place prepared by God, so that there she can be nourished for one thousand two hundred sixty days.

And war broke out in heaven; Michael and his angels fought against the dragon. The dragon and his angels fought back, but they were defeated, and there was no longer any place for them in heaven.

Reading 3: Revelation 17:1–6—"The Great Whore"

Then one of the seven angels who had the seven bowls came and said to me, "Come, I will show you and the judgment of the great whore who is seated on many waters, with whom the kings of the earth have committed fornication, and with the wine of whose fornication the inhabitants of the earth have become drunk. So he carried me away in the spirit into a wilderness, and I saw a woman sitting on a scarlet beast that was full of blasphemous names, and it had seven heads and ten horns. The woman was clothed in purple and scarlet, and adorned with gold and jewels and pearls, holding in her hand a golden cup full of abominations and the impurities of her fornication; and on her forehead was written a name, a mystery: "Babylon the great, mother of whores and of earth' abominations." And I saw that the woman was drunk with the blood of the witnesses to Jesus.

Reading 4: Revelation 21:1–3— "The Bride of the Lamb"

Then I saw a new heaven and a new earth; for the first heaven and the first earth had passed away, and the sea was no more. And I saw the holy city, the new Jerusalem, coming down out of heaven from God, prepared as a bride adorned for her husband. And I heard a loud voice from the throne saying, "See, the home of God is among mortals. He will dwell with them as their God; they will be his peoples, and God himself will be with them. . . .
"

Reflection: "Women of Persistent Resistance"

Voice 1:

I am Jezebel.

I am a woman prophet.

I am silenced because I am a woman who asserts her belief and speaks on behalf of her followers.

I am not ashamed of what I am doing. I believe I have the right to express my own desires and convictions. I am a woman of persistent resistance against male-dominated institutions who abhor women of leadership. But I will rise and be heard.

Voice 2:

I am the Woman Clothed with the Sun.

I am chosen by God to give birth to a male child.

But I was caught in the middle of a heavenly war between Michael and the Dragon. They took my child away from me because I am weak. I was banished to a desert for more than one thousand days. After I regained my strength, I was given the wings of an eagle. I am a woman of persistent resistance against wars and militarization that diminish my capacity to live and let live. But I will hold up a clenched fist in peace and solidarity.

Voice 3:

I am the Great Whore.

I represent the city of Babylon: filthy, immoral, full of abomination!

I prostitute with cities of great power. I create diplomatic relationships in the name of commercialism and material wealth.

I am looked down on as a sinful city that deserved to be destroyed. I was burned, thrown out, and left naked. I am hurting—and dying. I am a woman of persistent resistance against abusive and powerful governments who continuously oppress and exploit the weak and the poor. I will never let them touch my body again!

Voice 4:

I am the Bride.
I am destined to marry the Lamb of God.
I am immaculate, as pure as white snow, submissive and meek. I represent God's people, the New Heaven and Earth. I am a virgin—a woman whose sexuality is defined according to the standards set by patriarchy. I am sinless and righteous, but I am not free to explore the outside world. I am domesticated and tamed to set the best model for women. I am a woman of persistent resistance against stereotyping and women's confinement to homes and domestic chores. I will break this chain and free myself!

DOXOLOGY:
(*TUNE: "PRAISE GOD FROM WHOM ALL BLESSINGS FLOW"*)

O Loving God, your daughters raise
To life and to our Redeemer's praise
We sing prophetic women's power
Among us here in this very hour. Amen.[3]

CLOSING SONG

"Sarah's Song of Blessing" (words and music: Colleen Fulmer, 1989) *or*

"May the God of Hope Go with Us" (words: Alvin Schutmaat, 1984; v. 2: Fred Kaan, 1993; music: Argentine folk melody) *or*

"Go Forth for God" (words: J. R. Peacey, 1970; music: Genevan Psalter, 1551)

SENDING FORTH
(Individual readers: Read all.)

Leader: Go in peace and proclaim to the world the wonderful works of women spirit brought by God who has given us true liberation!

People: O God, inspire us (me) with your love,
challenge us (me) with your strength,
empower us (me) with your truth,
to live for life in the midst of death,
to make women triumph in their vision and hopes.

All: All the earth say, Amen!

The Sign of Peace and Solidarity

Notes

An Overview

1. John Dominic Crossan, *The Seven Storytellers of Faith: A Lenten Study Series* (videotape produced by United Methodist Communications, Nashville, Tenn.; Trinity Parish, N.Y.; and Berkeley Studio, The United Church of Canada, 1997).

2. Jean-Pierre Prevost, *How to Read the Apocalypse* (St. Paul University Press, Ott.: Novalis, 1991; first published in English by SCM Press Ltd.: London, 1993), 17.

3. Ibid., 19.

4. Susan R. Garrett, "Revelation," *The Women's Bible Commentary*, ed. Carol Newsom and Sharon Ringe (Louisville, Ky.: Westminster John Knox, 1992), 377–82.

Session 1

1. Norma Hardy, "Women's Creed," *The Ecumenical Decade 1988–1998: Churches in Solidarity with Women* (Geneva: WCC, 1998), 56. Used by permission.

Session 2

1. Unpublished prayer used by permission of Lin Dodds, Australia.

2. Miriam Therese Winter, "Huldah," *WomanWisdom* (New York: Crossroad, 1991), 307–08. Used by permission.

3. Pauline Viviano, "Huldah," *Anchor Bible Dictionary*, ed. David Noel Freedman III et al. (New York: Doubleday, 1992), 3:321. Used by permission.

4. William Eugene Phipps, *Assertive Biblical Women* (Westport, Conn.: Greenwood Press, 1992), 85.

5. Winter, *WomanWord: A Feminist Lectionary and Psalter* (New York: Crossroad, 1990), 218–19.

6. Walter A. Elwell et al., eds., *Baker Encyclopedia of the Bible* (Grand Rapids, Mich.: Baker Book House, 1988), 2:2058.

7. Ibid., 2:2059.

8. Susan R. Garrett, "Revelation," *The Women's Bible Commentary*, ed. Carol Newsom and Sharon Ringe (Louisville, Ky.: Westminster John Knox, 1992), 378.

9. Ibid., 379.

10. Elisabeth Schüssler Fiorenza, *Revelation: Vision of a Just World* (New York: Crossroad, 1991), 56. Used by permission.

11. Winter, *WomanWord*, 222–23.

12. Ibid., 221.

Session 3

1. Susan R. Garrett, "Revelation," *The Women's Bible Commentary*, ed. Carol Newsom and Sharon Ringe (Louisville, Ky.: Westminster John Knox, 1992), 379.

2. Elisabeth Schüssler Fiorenza, *Revelation: Vision of a Just World* (New York: Crossroad, 1991), 80. Used by permission.

3. From a sermon by Renate Rose, "The Struggle of Bringing to Birth," delivered at Union Theological Seminary, Dasmarinas, Cavite, Philippines, 13 December 1993.

4. Garrett, 379.

5. Schüssler Fiorenza, 80–81.

6. Joyce Hollyday, *Clothed with the Sun* (Louisville, Ky.: Westminster John Knox, 1994), 237–39. Used by permission.

7. Inspired by Renate Rose, "The Struggle of Bringing to Birth."

8. Miriam Therese Winter, *WomanWitness: A Feminist Lectionary and Psalter,* part 2 (New York: Crossroad, 1992), 328. Used by permission.

Session 4

1. Tina Pippin, "The Revelation to John," *Searching the Scriptures: A Feminist Commentary,* vol. 2, ed. Elisabeth Schüssler Fiorenza, et al. (New York: Cross-road, 1993), 123–26. Used by permission.

2. Elisabeth Schüssler Fiorenza, *Revelation: Vision of a Just World* (New York: Crossroad, 1991), 81. Used by permission.

3. Homer Hailey, *Revelation: An Introduction and Commentary* (Grand Rapids, Mich.: Baker Book House, 1979). Used by permission.

4. "ETAN to Protest Canadian Military Sales to Indonesia," *Peace and Environment News* 10, no. 8 (October 1995): 1. Used by permission.

5. Sr. Mary John Mananzan, ed., *Woman and Religion* (Manila: Institute of Women's Studies, St. Scholastica's College, 1988), 39. Used by permission.

6. Colleen Fulmer, "Rest in My Wings," *Cry of Ramah* (Albany, Calif.: The Loretto Spirituality Network, 1985), 25–26. Available from Loretto Spirituality Network; 725 Calhoun; Albany CA 94706. Used by permission.

7. Prayer of St. Teresa of Avila (1515–1582) in Fulmer, *Cry of Ramah*, 27.

Session 5

1. Unpublished prayer used by permission of Lin Dodds, Australia.

2. Penney Kome, *Women of Influence: Canadian Women and Politics* (Toronto: Doubleday Canada, 1985), 25–33. Used by permission.

3. Susan R. Garrett, "Revelation," *The Women's Bible Commentary*, ed. Carol Newsom and Sharon Ringe (Louisville, Ky.: Westminster John Knox, 1992), 380–81.

4. Ibid., 381.

5. Elisabeth Schüssler Fiorenza, *Revelation: Vision of a Just World* (New York:Crossroad, 1991), 98. Used by permission.

6. Ibid., 95.

7. From a summary based on Tina Pippin's "The Revelation to John," in *Searching the Scriptures: A Feminist Commentary*, vol. 2, ed. Elisabeth Schüssler Fiorenza, et al. (New York: Crossroad, 1993), 120.

8. Ibid.

9. Insights from group discussion contributed by Ferdinand Serra, United Methodist Pastor, Philippines, 1993. Used by permission.

10. Rene Parmar, "I Am a Woman," *Ecumenical Decade 1988–1998: Churches in Solidarity with Women* (Geneva, Switz.: WCC Publications, 1998), 63. Used by permission.

11. Miriam Therese Winter, *WomanWitness: A Feminist Lectionary and Psalter*, part 2 (New York: Crossroad, 1992), 86–87. Used by permission.

12. Ibid., 85.

Session 6

1. Miriam Therese Winter, *WomanWitness: A Feminist Lectionary and Psalter*, part 2 (New York: Crossroad, 1992), 331–32. Used by permission.

2. Contributed by Ferdinand Serra.

3. Debra Satz, "Markets in Women's Sexual Labor," *Ethics* 106 (October 1995): 63–66.

4. Ibid., 65–66.

5. Leonard Davis, *The Philippines: People, Poverty, and Politics* (London: Macmillan, 1987), 99.

6. Ibid., 103.

7. Winter, *WomanWord: A Feminist Lectionary and Psalter* (New York: Crossroad, 1990), 74.

8. Ibid., 73.

Session 7

1. Vjosa Dobruna, "Others on the List Were Not as Lucky," Testimonial Refugees, U.S. Committee for Refugees Web site <www.irsa-uscr.org>.

2. John Guimond, *The Silencing of Babylon: A Spiritual Commentary on the Revelation of John* (New York: Paulist Press, 1991), 90–95.

3. Andre Jacques, *The Stranger within Your Gates: Uprooted in the World Today* (Geneva, Switz.: WCC Publications, 1986), 54–60.

Notes

4. Julia Esquivel, "I Am No Longer Afraid of Death," *Ecumenical Decade 1988-1998: Churches in Solidarity with Women* (Geneva, Switz.: WCC Publications, 1998), back cover.

5. Martha Ann Kirk, "Women of the World," *Her Wings Unfurled*, ed. Colleen Fulmer and Martha Ann Kirk (Albany, Calif.: The Loretto Spirituality Network, 1989), 6. Available from Loretto Spirituality Network; 725 Calhoun; Albany CA 94706.

Session 8

1. Susan R. Garrett, "Revelation," *The Women's Bible Commentary*, ed. Carol Newsom and Sharon Ringe (Louisville, Ky.: Westminster John Knox, 1992), 381–82.

2. Elisabeth Schüssler Fiorenza, *Revelation: Vision of a Just World* (New York: Crossroad, 1991), 109–10.

3. Tina Pippin, "The Revelation to John," *Searching the Scriptures: A Feminist Commentary*, vol. 2, ed. Elisabeth Schüssler Fiorenza, et al. (New York: Crossroad, 1993), 118–19.

4. Lynne Bundesen, *The Woman's Guide To The Bible* (New York: Crossroad, 1993), 180.

5. Judy Marchand, an activist and a potter from Brandon, Manitoba, on the life of her mother, from *Faces of Feminism: Portraits of Women across Canada*, ed. Pamela Harris (Toronto: Second Story Press, 1992), 38. Used by permission.

6. Miriam Therese Winter, *WomanWord: A Feminist Lectionary and Psalter* (New York: Crossroad, 1990), 134.

Session 9

1. Elisabeth Schüssler Fiorenza, *Revelation: Vision of a Just World* (New York: Crossroad, 1991), 109–10. Used by permission.

2. Martha Ann Kirk and Coral Nunnery, "Cherishing the Earth," *Her Wings Unfurled*, ed. Colleen Fulmer and Martha Ann Kirk (Albany,

Calif.: The Loretto Spirituality Network, 1989), 8–10. Available from Loretto Spirituality Network; 725 Calhoun; Albany CA 94706. Used by permission.

3. Miriam Therese Winter, *WomanWitness: A Feminist Lectionary and Psalter*, part 2 (New York: Crossroad, 1992), 339. Used by permission.

4. Diann L. Neu, "Think Green: Hope for Planet Earth," *WaterWheel* 8, no. 1 (1995): 5. Diann Neu is the codirector and cofounder of WATER, the Women's Alliance for Theology, Ethics, and Ritual; 8035—13th St.; Silver Spring MD 20910. Phone: 301-589-2509. Fax: 301-589-3150. She writes regularly for the *WaterWheel*, WATER'S quarterly publication. Used by permission.

Session 10

1. Utopia is an imaginary place in Thomas More's *Utopia* (1516), a perfect political and social system, fairyland, paradise, heaven, promised land, and Shang-ri-la.

2. Tina Pippin, *Death and Desire: The Rhetoric of Gender in the Apocalypse of John* (Louisville, Ky.: Westminster John Knox Press, 1992), 37.

3. Ibid., 28.

4. Ibid., 107.

5. Anonymous, Untitled, *Kalinangan* 12, no. 1 (1992): 24. Used by permission.

6. Anonymous, "We Have A Dream," *Kalinangan* 12, no. 1 (1992): inside back cover. Used by permission.

7. Martha Ann Kirk and Coral -Nunnery, "Cherishing the Earth," *Her Wings Unfurled*, ed. Colleen Fulmer and Martha Ann Kirk (Albany, Calif.: The Loretto Spirituality Network, 1989), 34–35. Available from Loretto Spirituality Network; 725 Calhoun; Albany CA 94706. Used by permission.

8. Miriam Therese Winter, *WomanWord: A Feminist Lectionary and Psalter* (New York: Crossroad, 1990), 189. Used by permission.

Session 11

1. Miriam Therese Winter, *God with Us* (Nashville, Tenn.: Parthenon, 1979), 33. Used by permission.

2. Winter, *WomanWitness: A Feminist Lectionary and Psalter*, part 2 (New York: Crossroad, 1992), 30. Used by permission.

3. The words of the doxology were inspired by material written by Renate Rose in worship materials used in a service she organized at Union Theological Seminary, Dasmarinas, Cavite, Philippines, 13 December 1993.

Bibliography

Anonymous. "We Have a Dream." *Kalinangan.* Vol. 12. No. 1 (1992): inside back cover.

Bundesen, Lynne. *The Woman's Guide to the Bible.* New York: Crossroad, 1993.

Crossan, John Dominic. *The Seven Storytellers of Faith: A Lenten Study Series.* Series 1. United Methodist Communications, Nashville, Tennessee, Trinity Parish, New York and Berkeley Studio, The United Church of Canada, 1997.

Davis, Leonard. *The Philippines: People, Poverty, and Politics.* London: Macmillan, 1987.

Dobruna, Vjosa. "Others on the List Were Not as Lucky." Testimonial Refugees, U.S. Committee for Refugees. Web site <www.irsa-uscr.org>.

Elwell ,Walter A., et al., eds. *Baker Encyclopedia of the Bible.* Grand Rapids, Mich.: Baker Book House, 1988.

Esquivel, Julia. "I Am No Longer Afraid of Death." *Ecumenical Decade 1988–1998: Churches in Solidarity with Women.* Geneva, Switz.: WCC

Publications, 1998. Back cover.

"ETAN to Protest Canadian Military Sales to Indonesia." *Peace and Environment News* 10. No. 8 (October 1995): 1.

Fiorenza, Elizabeth Schüssler. *Revelation: Vision of a Just World.* Minneapolis: Augsburg Fortress Press, 1991.

Fiorenza, Elizabeth Schüssler, et al., eds. *Searching the Scriptures.* New York: Crossroad, 1993.

Freedman, David Noel, et al., ed. *Anchor Bible Dictionary.* New York: Doubleday, 1992.

Fulmer, Colleen, and Martha Ann Kirk. *Her Wings Unfurled.* Albany, Calif.: The Loretto Spirituality Network, 1989.

Guimond, John. *The Silencing of Babylon: A Spiritual Commentary on the Revelation of John.* New York: Paulist Press, 1991.

Hailey, Homer. *Revelation: An Introduction and Commentary.* Grand Rapids, Mich: Baker Book House, 1979.

Harris, Pamela, ed. *Faces of Feminism: Portraits of Women across Canada.* Toronto: Second Story Press, 1992.

Hollyday, Joyce. *Clothed with the Sun.* Louisville, Ky.: Westminster John Knox Press, 1994.

Jacques, Andre. *The Stranger within Your Gates: Uprooted in the World Today.* Geneva, Switz.: WCC Publications, 1986.

Kome, Penney. *Women of Influence: Canadian Women and Politics.* Toronto: Doubleday Canada; Garden City, N.Y.: Doubleday, 1985.

Mananzan, Sr. Mary John, ed. *Woman and Religion.* Manila: Institute of Women's Studies, 1988.

Neu, Diane L. "Think Green: Hope for Planet Earth." *WaterWheel* 8, no. 1 (1995): 5

Newsom, Carol A., and Sharon H. Ringe, eds. *The Women's Bible Commentary*. London: Westminster Press, 1992.

Parmar, Rene. "I Am a Woman." *Ecumenical Decade 1988–1998: Churches in Solidarity with Women*. Geneva, Switz.: WCC Publications, 1998. 56.

Phipps, William Eugene. *Assertive Biblical Women*. Westport, Conn.: Greenwood Press, 1992.

Pippin, Tina. *Death and Desire: The Rhetoric of Gender in the Apocalypse of John*. Louisville, Ky.: Westminster John Knox, 1992.

Prevost, Jean-Pierre. *How to Read the Apocalypse*. Ottawa: Novalis, 1991.

Satz, Debra. "Markets in Sexual Labor." *Ethics* 106. (October 1995): 6366.

Winter, Miriam Therese. *God with Us*. Nashville, Tenn.: Parthenon Press, 1979.
——. *WomanWisdom*. New York: Crossroad, 1991.
——. *WomanWitness: A Feminist Lectionary and Psalter*. Part 2. New York: Crossroad, 1992.
——. *WomanWord: A Feminist Lectionary and Psalter*. New York: Crossroad, 1990.

Music Resources

Fulmer, Colleen. *Cry of Ramah.* Albany, Calif.: The Loretto Spirituality Network, 1985.

Fulmer, Colleen, and Martha Ann Kirk. *Her Wings Unfurled.* Albany, Calif.: TheLoretto Spirituality Network, 1989.

Hobbs, R. Gerald, ed. *Songs for a Gospel People.* Winfield, B.C.: Wood Lake Books, 1987.

Hardy, Nancy E., and Leonard Lythgoe, co-chairs, Hymn and Worship Resource Committee. *Voices United: The Hymn and Worship Book of the United Church of Canada.* Etobicoke, Ont.: The United Church Publishing House, 1996.

Job, Reuben B., chair, Hymnal Revision Committee. *New Methodist Hymnal, The: Book of United Methodist Worship.* Nashville,Tenn.: The United Methodist Publishing House, 1997.

Kirk, Martha Ann, with Colleen Fulmer. *Celebrations of Biblical Women's Stories.* Kansas City, Mo.: Sheed and Ward, 1987.

Winter, Miriam Therese. *An Anthology of Scripture Songs.* Philadelphia: Medical Mission Sisters, 1982.
——. *God with Us.* Nashville, Tenn.: Parthenon Press, 1979.
——. *Woman Prayer, Woman Song.* Oak Park, Ill.: Meyer Stone Books, 1987.

Other Books from The Pilgrim Press

Bad Girls of the Bible
Exploring Women of Questionable Virtue

Barbara J. Essex

0-8298-1339-X/Paper/144 pages/$13.95

Designed as a fourteen-week study, *Bad Girls of the Bible* explores the Bible's accounts of traditionally misunderstood or despised women including Lot's wife, Delilah, Jezebel, Salome, and Sapphira, challenging traditional, patriarchal perspectives and offering fresh interpretations while making biblical exegesis understandable to the average layperson.

Daughters of Dignity
African Women in the Bible and the Virtues of Black Womanhood

LaVerne McCain Gill

0-8298-1373-X/Paper/176 pages/$16.95

To reclaim a connection with their deep ethical roots and moral heritage, African American women must learn the stories of strength, courage, and faith. *Daughters of Dignity* seeks to identify these virtues and trace their roots. LaVerne McCain Gill provides suggestions for self-evaluation and narratives on contemporary programs to success-fully reestablish an ethic of black womanhood in the community.

Jesus and Those Bodacious Women
Life Lessons from One Sister to Another

Linda H. Hollies

0-8298-1246-6/Paper/224 pages/$11.95

Linda Hollies serves up new spins on the stories of biblical women. From Eve to Mary Magdalene, portraits of the bodaciousness of the many matriarchs of the Christian tradition will prove to be blessings for readers. Study questions and examples of how one can grow in faith, spirituality, and courage—bodaciousness—are included at the end of each chapter.

Mother Goose Meets a Woman Called Wisdom
A Short Course in the Art of Self-determination

Linda H. Hollies

0-8298-1348-9/Cloth/142 pages/$21.95

Fairy tales will never be the same! Linda Hollies retells classic fairy tales with a decidedly spiritual spin. Hollies provides a guidebook for women at the crossroads of their lives by taking a look at biblical women. The results are a biblical approach to practicing the art of self-determination.

To order call The Pilgrim Press

800.537.3394

or visit

pilgrimpress.com